Payment Card Industry Professional (PCIP) V4.0

Your Ultimate Study Guide to Success

John Meah

CONTENTS

FOREWORD

Welcome to the exciting world of PCI-DSS! In today's digital age, keeping your organization safe from cyber threats is crucial. With new technologies emerging every day, it's vital to stay up-to-date with the latest version of the PCI-DSS standard to safeguard your organization against cyber criminals.

PCI-DSS version 4.0 will come into effect on March 31, 2024 as the only standard in use. The new version has 63 new requirements, with some effective immediately, but most won't be effective until March 31, 2025. This means businesses will have a year-long transition period to implement the more challenging requirements.

Note: the old PCIP v3.0 examination and its associated certification follow the **PCI-DSS v3.2.1 – this standard will be retired in March 2024.**

The new PCIP v4.0 training, examination, and associated certification will be available from September 2023.

For individuals obtaining the PCIP certification and adhering to the PCI-DSS standards, you will stand out from the competition to prospective employers. As an employer with staff certified to the new PCIP v4.0 standard, you can demonstrate to your customers that you take their security seriously.

Additionally, having a PCIP-certified employee on staff can give your business a competitive edge when it comes to winning contracts or partnerships with larger companies that require strict adherence to the PCI-DSS standards.

As the industry grows, keeping up with the latest standards and practices becomes increasingly important. I've got some great tips, summaries, and real-world examples to help you understand what it takes to become PCIP certified.

To earn your PCIP certification, you'll need to become an expert in critical areas related to PCI-DSS. But don't worry – with dedication and perseverance, you can prepare for the exam and gain the knowledge and skills you need to protect your customers' data.

This certification can truly advance your career and demonstrate your expertise in this critical technology area. So what are you waiting for? Let's get started on this exciting journey toward obtaining your PCIP v4.0 certification!

CHAPTER 1

OVERVIEW OF THE PCIP QUALIFICATION

Are you looking to take your knowledge of the payment card industry to the next level? Look no further than the PCIP 4.0 certification program offered by the Payment Card Industry Security Standards Council (PCI SSC). This certification will broaden your understanding of the payments ecosystem and widen your knowledge of payment card security.

Once you earn your PCIP certification, you can apply PCI Standards to support your organization's or clients' ongoing security and compliance efforts. One of the many benefits is being listed in the PCI SSC's searchable PCIP directory, where you can connect with other PCIPs and share valuable information and tips.

But that's not all - by earning your PCIP certification, you'll also become an expert in the essential set of security standards known as PCI-DSS, which will, in turn, enable you to protect cardholder data and reduce the risk of fraud.

Although earning your PCIP certification may be challenging, it's also a rewarding experience that requires effort, dedication, and expertise. It's an excellent opportunity for anyone looking to become a PCI-DSS expert! So take the time to study and prepare for this exciting journey that could open up a world of possibilities for you.

Application Process

Please note the following application process and examination details are correct at the time of publication. Please check the PCI SSC website for additional confirmation: https://www.pcisecuritystandards.org/

To become PCIP qualified, complete an online application form with the PCI SSC. It's a straightforward process where you'll outline your work experience, highlighting any experience with PCI-DSS. Once you've submitted your application, the PCI SSC will assess it and confirm their acceptance via email. They'll then forward your information to PearsonVUE, who will contact you via email to establish your user credentials. The whole process is quick and easy, taking only a few days to complete.

Tip: You have two options to choose from, Exam-only or instructor-led class. If you choose either of these options, you'll have a 30-day test window to complete the exam. Alternatively, if you opt for the eLearning Course, you'll have a generous 90-day test window to complete the exam. To optimize the time available to you, schedule your test towards the very last week of the 90 Days.

PearsonVUE is a true pioneer in the world of computer-based testing. With an array of online and proctored exams that demand a secure testing environment, Pearson VUE is all set to take your learning experience to the next level. You will join the thousands of satisfied candidates who have aced their exams with Pearson VUE's user-friendly digital testing platform, all from the comfort of your home. Of course, if you have access to a physical testing center, you can attend in person.

Tip: Checkout the PCI SSC website for current examination and course pricing: https://www.pcisecuritystandards.org/

Please note there are also in-person and eLearning courses available via the PCI SSC - check their website for details. Once you have been invoiced and paid the exam fee, you can log in to Pearson VUE to schedule your test day.

Tip: During the test, you will have access to a whiteboard where you can jot down notes to help jog your memory.

Examination

To prepare for the PCIP qualification, in tandem with reading this book, familiarize yourself with the PCI Standards and supporting documentation before taking the exam.

First things first, let's discuss the exam. As previously mentioned, PearsonVUE administers the PCIP exam, which comprises 75 multiple-choice questions that you will have 90 minutes to complete. Make sure you answer all questions, even if you're unsure of the correct answer, your best guess is better than leaving it blank.

Once you have completed the exam, you will receive either a **Pass** or **Fail** result. To pass, you must have answered at least 75% of the questions correctly. But with all the hard work and dedication you have put into your studies, I am confident you will come out on top!

Tip: Pearson VUE list the new version of the examination as PCIP 4.0: Payment Card Industry Professional.

Learning Objectives

Working through this study guide will help you develop a fundamental understanding of the payment card industry and the need to protect payment card data. Once you have reviewed the material in this book, revisit each chapter to become fully conversant with each subject area. Ensure that you also read through the official PCI-DSS v4.0 documents. The official documents contain a lot of information, and although you don't have to remember it verbatim, a high-level understanding will aid you considerably. You will find all the documents on the PCI SSC website: https://www.pcisecuritystandards.org/doc ument_library/

Doing this will ensure the following:

- You will be familiar with the PCI standards, understand the payment industry terminology, and understand the PCI Code of Professional Responsibility.

- You will develop an understanding of how PCI DSS applies to cardholder data and appreciate the intent of the PCI requirements.

- Knowing where to use the Self-Assessment Questionnaires (SAQs) will become second nature.

- You will learn about various resources, including the information supplements on the PCI SSC website.

- You will understand the impact of newer technologies like encryption, Wi-Fi, NFC, and Bluetooth on PCI compliance. You will also be able to articulate the PCI-DSS requirements concerning these new technologies.

- You will learn to determine the usage of Compensating Controls and locate additional information on them.

- By the end of your learning, you will have a comprehensive understanding of the six control objectives and their 12 requirements and a strong comprehension of the various sub-requirements, enabling you to recall and describe them.

As you progress through this study guide, you may observe that certain parts of the text are repeated multiple times. This intentional tactic is designed to strengthen the information in your memory.

Summary

The Payment Card Industry Security Standards Council offers the PCIP certification program to deepen your knowledge of the payments ecosystem and develop your payment card security knowledge. Once certified, individuals can apply PCI standards to support their organization's or clients' ongoing security and compliance efforts. The program also makes individuals experts in the essential set of security standards known as PCI-DSS, enabling them to protect cardholder data and reduce the risk of fraud. The certification process involves outlining work experience and passing an exam through Pearson VUE, either online or in person. The learning objectives include developing a fundamental understanding of the payment card industry, PCI standards, and how PCI DSS applies to cardholder data.

CHAPTER 2

ISA, QSA & PCIP: UNLOCKING THE PATH TO SUCCESS

If you want to advance your career in the payment card industry, several certifications can help you do just that. However, to give yourself the best possible chance of success, you should take a look at the PCI-QSA, PCI-ISA, and of course, the PCIP certification. These are the ones employers are looking for these days, and having them on your resume, either currently or historically, will set you apart from other candidates. By earning these certifications, you'll gain all the knowledge and skills you need to excel in this field. Plus, they'll give you a significant confidence boost and help you stand out from the crowd when it comes to landing your dream job.

PCI-ISA: Internal Security Assessor

Are you a part of an information security team in a small, medium or large merchant environment, acquiring bank, or processor? Do you want to enhance your knowledge of PCI Security Standards and ensure that your company meets the requirements of PCI DSS with ease and efficiency? Look no further than the Internal Security Assessor (ISA) Program! The PCI SSC approves this certification and provides rigorous training to professionals like you. By becoming an ISA, you play a crucial role in securing payment data and ensuring that your organization complies with data security standards. Something to be aware of is that the ISA certification is tied to your current employer. Still, if you move to a new employer, you can retake the ISA examination to maintain your certification.

PCI-QSA: Qualified Security Assessor

Are you familiar with the role of a Qualified Security Assessor (QSA)? QSAs are certified professionals who have completed an accredited course in PCI data security. The PCI SSC authorizes them to conduct assessments and ensure that organizations comply with PCI standards. But QSAs do more than evaluate an organization's compliance status. They'll work collaboratively with organizations to help them meet PCI DSS standards. By providing recommendations and guidance, QSAs help organizations remediate non-compliance issues and achieve PCI compliance.

If you're interested in becoming a QSA, you must be associated with a company that conducts PCI-DSS assessments to become a certified QSA. However, if you decide to part ways with your employer, your QSA certification will expire. But don't worry - if you plan to join another company as a qualified QSA, you can go through the recertification process and continue your career in this exciting field.

If you're already a QSA and looking for a new challenge, keep an eye out for job postings on LinkedIn! These roles are perfect for individuals contemplating a move to another company or wanting to continue working as QSAs. And the best part? Your new employer will likely cover the cost of recertification. So don't hesitate - take advantage of these exciting opportunities and continue making a difference as a Qualified Security Assessor!

PCIP: Payment Card Industry Professional

The Payment Card Industry Professional (PCIP 4.0) Program offered by the PCI SSC is a fantastic opportunity for professionals in the payment card industry to showcase their expertise in PCI-DSS Standards and supporting materials.

By obtaining this certification, practitioners can demonstrate their professional knowledge and understanding of the subject, which can help enhance their careers while staying up-to-date with the latest standards and practices.

The PCIP Qualification is a foundational certification demonstrating knowledge of the PCI standards and supporting materials. It focuses on relevant PCI-DSS fundamentals and critical areas of expertise required to become a trusted advisor to the payment card industry.

The PCIP certification is not just a valuable qualification but also a crucial stepping stone toward becoming an Internal Security Assessor (ISA) or a Qualified Security Assessor (QSA).

As someone who has worked in a large merchant environment where I established PCI-DSS compliance and now as a PCI-DSS specialist at an international offshore bank, I can attest to the importance of the PCIP credential.

Becoming a PCIP offers you a unique opportunity to comprehend the intricacies of the PCI-DSS Standards and their interrelatedness. The credential is valid for three years, and as long as you meet the Continuing Professional Education (CPE) requirement, it remains with you for life.

A basic understanding of information technology, network security, and architecture is required before taking the PCIP examination. Candidates are highly recommended to undertake the PCIP training course(s) provided by the PCI SSC to enhance their knowledge and increase their chances of success in the examination.

Summary

This chapter discussed three certifications that can help professionals advance their careers in the payment card industry: PCI-QSA, PCI-ISA, and PCIP. PCI-ISA is for information security team members who want to enhance their knowledge of PCI Security Standards and ensure their company meets requirements. PCI-QSA is for those associated with a company conducting PCI-DSS assessments. PCIP is for professionals in the payment card industry to showcase their expertise in PCI-DSS Standards and supporting materials. All three certifications require passing an examination and may require additional training courses. Obtaining these certifications can help professionals stand out in the job market and enhance their knowledge of data security standards.

CHAPTER 3

THE EVOLUTION OF THE PAYMENT CARD INDUSTRY

The PCI Security Standards Council (PCI SSC) is a global non-profit organization established in 2006. Their main goal is to oversee the creation, management, education, and promotion of the worldwide PCI security standards. They are dedicated to ensuring that payment transactions worldwide are secure and protected. They have been instrumental in creating and raising awareness about these standards, which is a huge deal in today's world, where cybercrime is rampant.

The major credit card companies, including Visa, MasterCard, American Express, Discover, JCB and UnionPay, have come together to make their data security compliance programs more effective by adopting the PCI-DSS. This standard provides a comprehensive set of guidelines for merchants and service providers who handle sensitive cardholder data. By implementing the PCI-DSS, organizations can take steps to secure their cardholder data environments (CDE).

The Payment Card Industry-Data Security Standard (PCI-DSS) is always up-to-date with industry trends and practices. It's an incredible resource for businesses that want to accept credit card payments safely. The PCI DSS v4.0 Quick Reference Guide and the PCI Security Standards Council website are helpful resources for anyone who wants to learn more about this standard.

Tip: You can access the guide via this link: PCI-DSS Quick Reference Guide.and visit the PCI SSC website via this link: PCI Security Standards Council

Every organization that processes these payments must comply with the standard, as failure to do so can lead to penalties or even the suspension of payment processing privileges. The good news is that the PCI Council not only mandates adherence to the PCI-DSS but also offers advice and help to those who need it.

The council provides extensive training programs for individuals, merchants, and service providers who must comply with PCI-DSS. They also offer certification and validation services to ensure that organizations meet compliance requirements. So if you're looking for a way to keep your customers' information safe and secure while accepting credit card payments, ensure that you comply with the PCI-DSS.

PCI-DSS

Have you ever wondered how your credit card information is kept safe when purchasing? The answer lies in the Payment Card Industry Data Security Standard (PCI-DSS). This comprehensive set of security standards was established in 2004 through a collaboration between the PCI Security Standards Council and the American National Standards Institute (ANSI).

To ensure that organizations maintain compliance with PCI-DSS, they must meet a series of requirements to establish a secure payment card processing environment. These requirements include implementing robust security controls and monitoring and reporting security incidents. Additionally, organizations must ensure that their network architecture and software design meet stringent security standards.

By adhering to these requirements, organizations can provide customers with peace of mind and demonstrate their commitment to protecting sensitive data. The PCI-DSS represents a vital framework for ensuring the safety and security of credit card information. So next time you make a purchase with your credit card, rest assured that measures are in place to keep your data safe and secure.

Payment Card Industry Data Security Standard Version: 4.0

The PCI-DSS Version Timeline

Version	Release Date
Version 1	December 2004
Version 1.1	September 2006
Version 1.2	October 2008
Version 2.0	October 2010
Version 3.0	November 2013
Version 3.1	April 2015
Version 3.2	April 2016
Version 3.2.1	May 2018
Version 4.0	March 2022

Version Timeline

PROMOTE SECURITY AS A CONTINUOUS PROCESS

Security testing has to be a continuous process, business as usual (BAU), rather than a snapshot of an organization's PCI DSS compliance taken once a year during the annual audit. Documentation tells assessors (QSAs) that they must select samples over a period of time to prove compliance.

In order to keep our sensitive information and financial data safe, it's important to understand that security testing is not a one-time event. It's a continuous process that should be ongoing throughout the year, rather than just during the annual audit. This helps ensure that our organization is always meeting the PCI DSS compliance standards and staying up-to-date with any changes.

To prove that we are compliant with PCI DSS version 4.0, we need to provide evidence of our security measures over a period of time. This means that we can't just rely on a single snapshot of our security practices but must instead demonstrate our ongoing commitment to security.

By treating security as a continuous process, we can help protect our organization from potential threats and keep our customers' data secure. So let's ensure we're always vigilant and taking the necessary steps to maintain our security standards.

ENHANCE VALIDATION METHODS AND PROCEDURES

The new and improved version 4.0 of the PCI DSS, has made some exciting changes to its authentication requirements to ensure the security of your data. We all know that passwords are the key to keeping our accounts safe. Therefore, the new standards now require passwords to be at least 12 characters long, and they must contain a mix of numbers and letters. This means that you can no longer use simple passwords like "1234" or "password" as your security code. Instead, you need to come up with something more complex and unique to ensure that your account stays secure.

But wait, there's more! To make sure that your data is even more secure, multi-factor authentication (MFA) will now become mandatory for all accounts that provide access to the card data environment. This means that you will need to verify your identity using more than one method, such as a password and a fingerprint scan or a security token. By using MFA, we can ensure that only authorized users can access the cardholder data, which is an essential step in keeping the information secure.

In conclusion, the new authentication requirements in PCI DSS version 4.0 are designed to enhance validation methods and procedures to reflect the latest industry best practices. By using longer passwords and multi-factor authentication, we can all work together to keep our data safe and secure. See User Authentication and Password Security in Chapter 26for a deep dive.

ADD FLEXIBILITY AND SUPPORT OF ADDITIONAL METHODOLOGIES TO ACHIEVE MORE STRINGENT SECURITY REQUIREMENTS

The latest version of PCI DSS, version 4.0, has made a significant change that gives organizations more freedom to create their own controls and put them into action. This is a big deal because it means companies can be more flexible in adopting new technologies or security solutions to meet compliance requirements. For instance, they can now use cloud-based hosting services without worrying about complicated language or confusing intent statements. This opens up a whole new world of possibilities for businesses looking to stay ahead of the curve and protect their payment security. Some examples of these different technologies include mobile payments, biometric authentication, and tokenization. With these tools at their disposal, companies can rest assured that they're doing everything possible to keep their customers' data safe and secure.

Summary

When protecting our credit card information, we all want peace of mind. Fortunately, there's a framework in place that's always on top of the latest industry trends and practices - the Payment Card Industry Data Security Standard (PCI-DSS 4.0). By following these requirements, businesses can show their commitment to safeguarding sensitive data and give customers the reassurance they need. It's a must for any organization handling credit card payments, and non-compliance can lead to penalties or even losing the ability to process payments. Luckily, the PCI Security Standards Council offers training and certification services to help businesses stay compliant. So next time you swipe your card, rest easy knowing your data is in good hands.

CHAPTER 4

THE PAYMENT BRANDS

The Six Card Brands

Meet the six powerhouse brands that are behind PCI-DSS Compliance:

1. American Express

2. Discover Financial Services

3. JCB International

4. MasterCard Worldwide

5. Visa International

6. UnionPay

Payment Brand Compliance Programs

Each of the six payment brands develops and maintains its own PCI DSS compliance program under its security risk management policies. However, all PCI DSS requirements are common to all PCI DSS-compliant organizations.

- Visa Inc: Cardholder Information Security Program (CISP).

- Visa Europe: Account Information Security (AIS) Program.

- Mastercard: Site Data Protection (SDP).

- American Express: Data Security Operating Policy (DSOP).

- JCB International: Data Security Program.

- UnionPay: In 2020, UP became a strategic member of the PCI Security Standards Council (PCI SSC).

The payment brand compliance programs encompass a set of responsibilities crucial to ensure adherence to regulations and standards. These duties are not only essential but also fascinating to understand:

- Tracking and enforcement.

- Penalties, fees, compliance deadlines.

- Validation process and who needs to validate.

- Approval and posting of compliant entities.

- Definition of merchant and service provider levels.

Payment Brand Roles

Six big brands that ensure businesses maintain top-notch security standards guard the world of payment processing. These brands are the ultimate authority regarding PCI-DSS compliance and accept validation documentation from only the most trusted QSAs and ASV companies. They give their seal of approval only to those who have met the rigorous qualifications. The payment brands hold a crucial position in the PCI-DSS compliance process as they assess the quality of validation documentation, ensuring it meets their high standards.

Payment brands have a crucial role in defining rules for forensic analysis to address data breaches. They provide oversight and support investigations of account data compromises. To learn more about payment brands, check out the PCI SSC website and read FAQ 1142. There, you'll find a list of contacts you need to get in touch with different payment brands, along with helpful information on what to do if a data breach occurs. You'll also find a list of security do's and don'ts to help you stay safe while making online payments.

The six payment brands play an important role in ensuring that businesses and consumers are protected by maintaining their PCI-DSS compliance. They grant a seal of approval to those who have completed the rigorous validation process. Payment brands serve as the guardians of account data security, providing oversight and support in the unfortunate event of a data breach.

Summary

Five of the biggest payment brands in the world established the Payment Card Industry Security Standards Council: American Express, Discover Financial Services, JCB International, MasterCard Worldwide, and Visa International (UnionPay is a recent addition). Each brand has a unique data security compliance program and responsibilities adhering to the PCI-DSS. These include monitoring and enforcing security measures, imposing penalties and fees for non-compliance, carrying out validation processes, and defining the levels of merchants and service providers. The payment brands are not just figureheads - they play a critical role in ensuring that all validation documentation is of high quality and in responding to data breaches. Think of them as guardians who closely monitor account data to ensure that all security standards are met.

THE HIDDEN DANGERS OF IGNORING THE PCI-DATA SECURITY STANDARD

In today's digital age, cybercriminals are always on the look out for backdoors or weaknesses in payment systems. They aim to exploit any vulnerability they find to gain access to valuable financial resources and sensitive data.

As technology advances, so do the tactics of cybercriminals. It's crucial to stay alert and informed about the potential dangers lurking in the digital world. By implementing the PCI-DSS, you can equip your organization with the tools to tackle these threats and safeguard your valuable cardholder data. Through this forward-thinking approach, you can stay one step ahead, ensuring that your security measures are always current.

The Bull's Eye: Payment Card Data in the Crosshairs of Cybercriminals

Payment card data is a prime target for cybercriminals; they can misuse it to deceive and steal funds from cardholders. The industries most vulnerable to hacker attacks include retail, information services, financial organizations, food services, hospitality, and accommodation.

In the world of cybersecurity, there is a silent but dangerous threat lurking around - stolen credentials. According to Verizon's Data Breach Investigation Report 2017, almost all data breaches (95%) involving stolen credentials use vendor remote access to sneak into their customers' point of sale (PoS) systems. It gives malicious actors an easy way to steal valuable data and wreak havoc on unsuspecting businesses.

Credit card fraud has become a severe problem in the United States, with over 1.4 million reported cases in 2021 alone. The losses incurred by businesses and consumers due to credit card fraud were estimated to be around $10 billion in 2022. This staggering amount highlights the need for more robust security measures to safeguard consumers and merchants.

These statistics are a sobering reminder that even the most minor vulnerability in your security can have devastating consequences.

The good news is businesses can take action to safeguard themselves against such attacks. By implementing robust authentication protocols and closely monitoring vendor access, companies can rest assured that only authorized personnel can access their PoS systems. It's also crucial for businesses to regularly audit their systems to ensure that no unauthorized access has been granted. By implementing these security measures, companies can effectively shield themselves from the danger of stolen credentials and keep their customers' valuable data secure.

The latest version of PCI-DSS, version 4.0, will incorporate the latest security technologies and best practices to protect against emerging threats. For example, version 4.0 will require merchants to implement multi-factor authentication for all access to the cardholder data environment (CDE) to prevent unauthorized access.

Another significant change in version 4.0 is the emphasis on risk management. Merchants will be required to conduct regular risk assessments to identify potential vulnerabilities and take appropriate measures to address them.

Overall, PCI-DSS version 4.0 is a significant step forward in the fight against credit card fraud. By incorporating the latest security technologies and best practices and emphasizing risk management, the new standard will help reduce losses and safeguard merchants and consumers alike. All merchants must comply with the new guidelines to ensure the security of credit card transactions and protect against emerging threats.

Unlocking the Mystery: How is Data Targeted?

The era of technology has created many opportunities for criminals to extract valuable data sneakily. It's akin to a thief slipping away under cover of darkness with your most prized possessions. As certified PCIPs, we ensure that these malevolent individuals cannot get away with their nefarious acts. To defend against attacks, we must stay current with PCI controls and requirements to protect the CDE from digital thieves.

Unfortunately, criminals nowadays have access to a plethora of tools they can use to snatch your valuable information. These tools are accessible online, making it easier for them to commit crimes. To make matters worse, these criminals even form online communities to share data and information.

The Art of Deception: How Phishing Puts Your Business at Risk

Phishing, a social engineering tactic, involves sending you a message that appears to come from a trustworthy source, such as your bank, Facebook, or another provider. They may ask for your login credentials or other personal information. You could fall for the scam and lose your data if you're not careful. These criminals are clever and will do whatever it takes, using reconnaissance and social engineering tools to get their hands on your private information.

Have you ever received an email and clicked on a link that redirected you to a website, only to find out later that it was a scam? This is called phishing, and it's a sneaky way for cybercriminals to steal your private information, like credit card numbers, passwords, and personal identification numbers. Cybercriminals using social engineering tactics such as phishing are experts at tricking people into thinking they're trustworthy businesses or reputable individuals. They use many tactics to make their emails and websites look real, but they're just trying to steal your money or identity. Don't fall victim to these scams - stay vigilant and protect your personal information at all costs!

Card Skimming

One example of these tools is the magnetic card reader, which can swiftly steal your data. Another is the software used for writing sensitive information from cloned cards, which are widely available on the internet and can even be got for free.

Have you ever come across the term skimming device? Well, it's a technique criminals use to steal credit or debit card information. They do this by copying the data off the magnetic strip on your card. To carry out this sneaky act, they use skimming devices which they place over the card reader on the front of the terminal. Once you insert your card, these devices capture and copy the data strip to a computer. It's essential to be aware of these devices and watch for them!

Criminals who steal payment card data interfere with things like PoS devices, ATMs, and Kiosks. The scary part is it's tough to spot the difference between the real thing and a fake fascia that the bad guys put there. Keep your eyes peeled!

It's been found that criminals can infiltrate retail stores and other places that use point-of-sale (PoS) devices. They will land trusted positions behind the counter where they can't be seen using small skimming devices like the ones shown here. It's a serious issue that demands vigilance!

Skimming Devices small enough to fit in the palm of your hand

This is the full kit of card read\write software, complete with cards

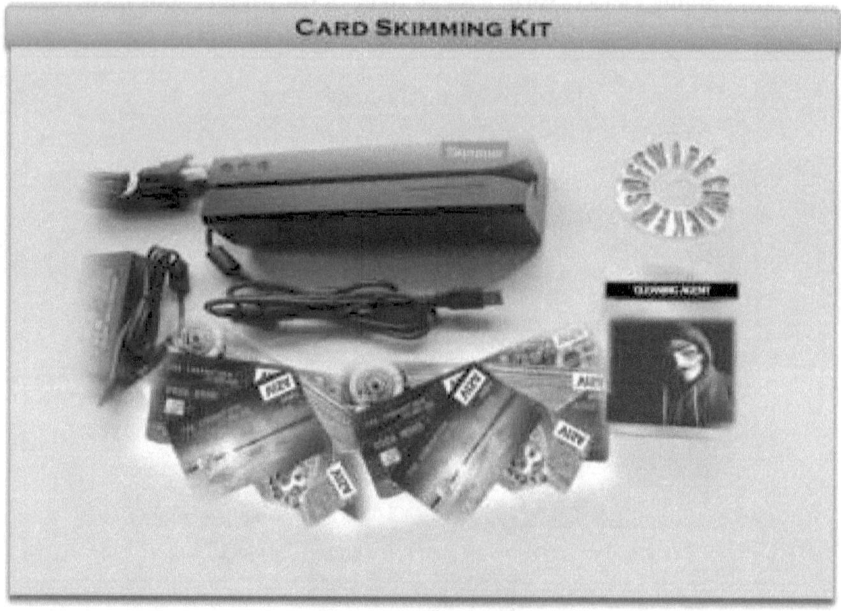

These crafty devices copy the magnetic stripe on your card, which can create fraudulent cloned cards for online purchases. Shockingly, skimming costs an estimated $2 billion worldwide!

In today's digital age, the security of sensitive information has become more crucial than ever. Criminals are always on the lookout to get your card data, which they can sell on the Dark Web to other fraudsters. Other criminals can use this captured data to make fraudulent transactions without having physical cards, commonly known as eCommerce or mail-order/telephone order transactions (MOTO). Criminals will go to great lengths to steal cardholder data (CHD) and sensitive authentication data (SAD) and then sell them in bulk to other criminals who will use this information to commit their crimes. It is imperative for any organization that accepts payments via credit or debit card to prioritize the security of CHD, as no organization is immune to these malicious attacks.

It's crucial to have qualified PCIPs on your team. They protect your data, shielding it from the harmful intentions of cyber criminals. With their knowledge and skills, you can be confident that your customers' data is in excellent hands, and you can focus on growing your business without worrying about security breaches.

Mobile payments have become increasingly popular, and one of the most commonly used methods is contactless card payments. You only need an electronic payment card with a contactless chip to use this method. It's as simple as holding the card up to the contactless reader on the merchant's device when making a purchase. Quick and easy. But wait, you should know some security risks associated with this payment method.

As already mentioned, card skimming is a common threat where thieves can steal your card information by reading the data off the card while you make a purchase. Second, there is also a risk of card cloning. It happens when a thief creates a fake card that contains your sensitive authentication data (SAD) and uses it to make contactless payments, giving them access to your money. So, while convenient, it's essential to remember these risks when using contactless card payments.

Tip: Several methods for stealing payment card data exist, including physical skimming, malware, and weak passwords. In addition, criminals are now able to inject skimming code into e-commerce sites.

Malware

Malware can cause severe damage to your computer system. It comes in various forms, including worms, viruses, trojans, spyware, adware, and rootkits. Spyware and adware are particularly harmful, as they can steal sensitive information and bombard you with unwanted ads. Worms and viruses spread quickly and can take down an entire system.

Let's talk about how malware can affect PCI-DSS in the context of credit cards.

Imagine you're a small business owner who accepts credit card payments from customers. You have out-of-date anti-malware software installed on your computer system, and one day you receive an email with an attachment from what appears to be a legitimate source. You open the attachment and unknowingly download malware onto your system.

This malware is designed to steal credit card information from your customers as they make purchases on your website. Without even realizing it, you've become vulnerable to a data breach that could compromise your customers' sensitive information.

This is where PCI-DSS comes into play. The standard requires businesses to implement measures to protect against malware attacks, such as regularly updating anti-malware software and conducting vulnerability scans. Failure to comply with these requirements can result in hefty fines and damage your reputation as a business owner.

It's important to stay alert and take steps to defend against malicious software. Keep your anti-virus and anti-malware software up-to-date. Educate yourself and your employees on how to identify and avoid potential threats.

Protecting against malware is essential to maintaining PCI-DSS compliance when accepting credit card payments. Don't let pesky malware programs compromise your customers' sensitive information - stay secure!

Unveiling the Hidden Danger: The Insider Threat to PCI-DSS Compliance

Did you know that one of the greatest threats to a company's security comes from within the company itself? That's right; the insider threat is a real danger that can compromise sensitive data and put your business at risk.

Let's break it down. An insider threat is when someone within the company, such as an employee or contractor, intentionally or unintentionally causes harm to the organization. In the context of PCI-DSS compliance, this could mean an employee mishandling credit card information, stealing data, or even selling it on the dark web.

So why is this such a big deal? Well, not only does it put your customers' personal and financial information at risk, but it can also result in hefty fines and damage your business's reputation. In fact, according to a recent study by IBM, the average cost of a data breach in 2020 was $3.86 million!

To give you an idea of what can happen, let's consider the real-world example of the Target data breach in 2013. Hackers were able to steal credit card information from over 40 million customers by exploiting vulnerabilities in Target's payment system.

However, it was later discovered that the hackers gained access by compromising the credentials of an HVAC contractor who had access to Target's network.

This incident illustrates how important it is to secure not only your systems but also those of any third-party vendors or contractors with access to sensitive data.

While PCI-DSS compliance is crucial for protecting credit card information, it's also essential to be conscious of the insider threat. Implementing proper security measures such as strong access controls, regularly reviewing and updating security protocols, and conducting thorough background checks on contractors and vendors. Furthermore, teaching staff how to correctly manage confidential information can help protect your business from security breaches.

Summary

This chapter discussed the importance of implementing PCI-DSS guidelines to protect against potential threats to cardholder data. Cybercriminals often target payment card data and use various methods, such as skimming, phishing, malware, and contactless payment fraud, to steal sensitive information. Insider threats are also significant, where employees mishandle or steal credit card information. It is crucial to secure not only your systems but also those of any third-party vendors or contractors with access to sensitive data. Implementing robust authentication protocols, closely monitoring vendor access, and conducting thorough background checks on contractors and vendors can help safeguard valuable cardholder data. Failure to comply with these requirements can result in hefty fines and damage your reputation as a business owner.

CHAPTER 6

UNVEILING THE INTRICACIES OF THE PAYMENT CARD ECOSYSTEM

Have you ever stopped to think about how often we rely on payment cards in our daily lives? It's all possible thanks to the payment card ecosystem - a vast network of institutions and companies working together to streamline card transactions. Banks, credit card companies, and merchants are just a few players in this ecosystem. They collaborate to create a seamless platform for merchants to accept card payments and for we cardholders to make purchases easily. It is fascinating how this system works so seamlessly in the background, allowing us to focus on what matters - enjoying our purchases!

The payment card network is the backbone of the global economy, creating a seamless system for processing payments. Thanks to this incredible technology, we can now easily shop for goods and services worldwide. But how does it all come together? What makes it so successful? And what challenges does it face? Join me as we delve into the fascinating world of payment cards and other players.

Understanding the payment card ecosystem is essential to succeed in the PCIP exam and beyond. This knowledge will equip you with the tools you need to evaluate potential risks confidently.

The payment card industry is a complicated web of interconnected parts, all working together seamlessly to keep the system running smoothly. To ace the exam, you need to comprehend how each component interacts with one another.

A deep understanding of the payment card system is crucial when working with organizations that handle cardholder data. This knowledge will prove invaluable in assessing and managing compliance risks. With this insight, you'll be able to make informed decisions on how best to safeguard cardholder data and ensure that your organization remains compliant with the PCI-DSS standard. It's essential to keep this in mind as you work towards test day.

The payment card ecosystem includes the following key stakeholders:

Cardholders

Imagine this: you and I, along with countless others, are the proud owners of debit and credit cards. These little plastic powerhouses are the key to unlocking our hard-earned cash when we hit the supermarket or make purchases online. We cardholders are the drivers of the economic engine! We keep the wheels turning and the economy humming with a simple swipe or tap. So don't underestimate the power of those trusty cards in your wallet–they are worth their weight in gold!

Issuers

Issuers, also known as Banks, provide you with the magical debit and credit cards. They are your trusted allies, providing a range of financial services to help you manage your money safely and efficiently. HSBC to Citibank, NatWest to American Express - these issuers are the lifeblood of the financial system, providing you with access to your funds and the ability to make purchases. In short, issuers are essential to your financial journey, paving the way for a brighter and more secure financial future.

Tip: American Express (AMEX), is the only card brand that issues cards directly to customers.

Merchants

When we buy goods or services, whether online or in physical stores, we can use our credit or debit cards to make payments. Think of your favorite shopping places, like your go-to supermarket or trendy boutiques. These businesses fall under the merchant or retailer category.

In today's world of evolving technologies, potential risks are everywhere. That's why merchants must understand this reality and prioritize offering their customers a hassle-free and secure payment process. To achieve this, merchants should stay up-to-date on the latest secure payment technologies and security protocols so their customers can shop confidently and safely.

Acquirers

Merchants need help to process payments and manage their finances, and that's where Acquirers or Banks come in: HSBC, Citibank, and NatWest, as well as payment processors such as WorldPay and GlobalPay (among many others), offer merchants a range of financial tools and services, making it easier for them to do business.

Are you aware that banks like HSBC, NatWest, and Citibank and processors such as WorldPay and GlobalPay all provide merchants with tools for safely processing payments? Merchants could not accept payments securely without these acquiring banks and payment processors. These acquirers provide electronic payment devices, usually positioned at the checkout counter or self-service areas. So, the next time you make a purchase, remember these essential providers' roles in keeping your transactions safe and hassle-free.

Payment Brands

The world of payment brands can be overwhelming, but fear not! Six prominent payment brands act as the sturdy pillars of a castle for PCI DSS. These include Visa, Mastercard, American Express, Discover, JCB and more recently, UnionPay. If you have a debit or credit card from any of these brands, you're in expert hands regarding PCI-DSS compliance.

When you're making a purchase using a card with one of these five payment brands and the merchant uses a payment device that accepts payments from these brands, then PCI-DSS will apply to your transaction. Think of PCI-DSS as your knight in shining armor, protecting your data from malicious actors who may try to steal it. With PCI-DSS guarding your information, you can rest assured that your data is secure.

Tip: PCI-DSS Compliance Standards apply to Merchants, Acquirers, Issuers, card manufacturers, and processors involved in the Payment card ecosystem. All entities storing, processing, and transmitting cardholder information must comply with PCI-DSS.

Summary

The world of payment cards is a bustling network of institutions and companies working together to secure transactions. This ecosystem involves banks, credit card companies, and merchants collaborating to create a platform for seamless card payments. This system allows shoppers to use their cards to make purchases, while merchants can easily accept them. The payment card network also plays a crucial role in processing payments, which is an essential part of the global economy. The key players in this ecosystem include cardholders, issuers\banks, acquirers\banks, and the six payment brands: Visa, Mastercard, Discover, JCB, UnionPay and American Express. Understanding this ecosystem is vital for managing PCI compliance risks and acing the PCIP exam.

CHAPTER 7

THE PUZZLE OF CONNECTIONS: UNDERSTANDING HOW IT ALL FITS TOGETHER

Acquiring Bank

This bank holds business or merchants' funds. An Acquirer will offer them card readers to enable merchants to accept card payments. These nifty devices are used to process credit card transactions. The Acquiring bank will deposit the funds into the merchant's account once the transaction is completed. This means merchants can receive customer payments quickly and securely without worrying about handling cash or cheques. If you are a merchant looking to expand your payment options, getting established with a card reader is the way to go!

Tip: Examples of Acquirers are HSBC, NatWest, Santander, Bank of America and many others.

Payment Brands

Payment brands play a crucial role in facilitating transaction data transfers between issuing banks and merchants. They have the authority to set interchange rates and assessment fees, which significantly impact the cost of transactions. So, they are a big deal!

Tip: The leading global payment brands form a network connecting major banks worldwide: Visa, Mastercard, American Express, Discover, JCB and UnionPay.

Interchange Rates

Interchange rates are fees charged by payment brands for processing transactions between issuing banks and merchants. These rates vary depending on the type of card used, the transaction amount, and other factors. Understanding these interchange rates is crucial for merchants as they significantly impact the cost of accepting card payments and can affect their bottom line.

Assessment Fees

Assessment fees are additional charges imposed by payment brands for their services. These fees are separate from interchange rates and are charged to merchants for each transaction processed. Assessment fees vary depending on the payment brand and can include charges for network access, fraud prevention, and other services. Merchants should be aware of these assessment fees, which can add up quickly and impact their overall cost of accepting card payments.

Tip: The issuing bank verifies the cardholder's identity and confirms whether there are sufficient funds are available to cover the transaction.

Issuing Bank

Are you aware that as a cardholder, you have access to more than just an account with this bank? You can also open a current or savings account or even a mortgage account with them! This bank has got you covered with various financial services to meet your needs. When you use your card for a transaction, the issuing bank will verify that you have sufficient funds to complete it. Once confirmed, the bank will release the funds to settle the transaction.

Merchants

In the world of payment cards, merchants or retailers accept cards with logos from American Express, Discover, JCB, Mastercard, and Visa. These businesses can be online or in traditional brick-and-mortar premises. Merchant accounts are essential to the payment card ecosystem because they drive growth in the industry. Merchants who accept cards from all five members of the PCI SSC generate the most spending and are the driving force behind this growth.

Summary

This content explains the different players involved in the payment card ecosystem, including the acquiring bank, payment brands, interchange rates, assessment fees, issuing banks, and merchants. The acquiring bank holds a merchant's funds and offers them card readers to process credit card transactions. Payment brands set interchange rates and assessment fees that impact transaction costs. Interchange rates are fees charged for processing transactions between issuing banks and merchants, while assessment fees are additional charges for payment brand services. The issuing bank verifies the cardholder's identity and confirms sufficient funds to complete a transaction. Merchants accept cards from various payment brands and drive growth in the industry.

CHAPTER 8

UNLOCKING THE SECRETS OF THE CARD PAYMENT PROCESS

When you shop online or visit a store, a fascinating process unfolds. First, you get to pick the items that catch your eye. Once you've made your selections, it's time to head to the cashier with your shopping basket in tow. This is where the magic happens! You'll be asked to present your credit or debit card, which your bank issued. Then comes the exciting part - payment! You can use contactless payment by simply tapping your card or inserting/swiping it at the merchant's point of sale (POS) device. The bank provides this device with which the merchant does business, also known as their acquirer.

- Once you slide in your credit card and punch in your unique PIN, they process your payment instantly, taking only a few seconds to complete. It is like a mini adventure that concludes with a successful transaction.

- In the blink of an eye, a series of crucial steps guarantees a seamless transaction. These steps include securing the merchant's payment, accurately billing you for the goods or services, and safeguarding your credit card information from threats. This ultra-quick process is designed to make your purchasing experience effortless and secure.

Authorization

1. When it's time to settle the bill, the cardholder confidently approaches the PoS device at the front of the merchant or retailer's store. With a simple swipe or tap of their trusty credit or debit card, the payment is processed seamlessly and securely. No need to fumble for cash or count out coins - this modern method makes paying a breeze!

2. When you make a purchase using your card, the information is transmitted through the internet or by phone to the acquiring bank, its processor, or service provider. This ensures that your payment is processed quickly and securely, giving you peace of mind while you shop. So go ahead, swipe that card, and enjoy your purchase with confidence!

3. When you make a payment using your credit card, the payment brand network gets all the juicy details from the bank that processes your transaction. They're like detectives, analyzing the Track 1 and Track 2 data to determine who issued your card. And get this - they can even tell which bank it came from just by looking at the first few digits of your card! So next time you swipe that plastic, remember that an entire team of people is working behind the scenes to keep your transaction secure.

4. When you pay using your card, a special request is sent to the bank that issued your card. This request is made through a network of payment brands that work tirelessly behind the scenes to ensure your transaction is smooth and secure. It's like a secret handshake between your bank and the payment brand network - one that guarantees your payment is authorized and processed efficiently.

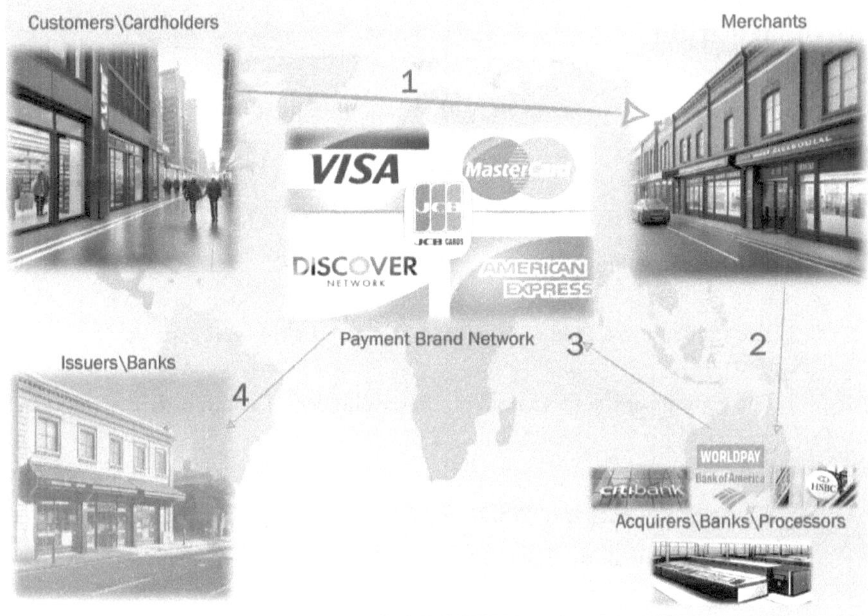

Authorization

Authentication

1. The Issuing Bank receives an Authorization Request from the Payment Brand network.

2. The Issuing Bank validates the credit card number, checks the available funds, matches the billing address, and validates the CVV.

3. The transaction is then Approved or Declined by the issuing bank.

4. The issuing bank places a hold on the cardholder's account until the amount is cleared.

5. At the end of each day (EoD), the merchant will perform an (EoD) task on the PoS terminal; the EoD task will collect all approved authorizations to be processed in a batch.

6. Once the transaction is completed, the merchant ensures the customer has a record of their purchase. They produce the record in one of two ways: by providing a printed receipt, which can be held in the customer's hand as a tangible reminder of their transaction, or by sending an electronic receipt via email to the cardholder's email address. This way, customers can keep track of their purchases and have a record of their transactions at their fingertips.

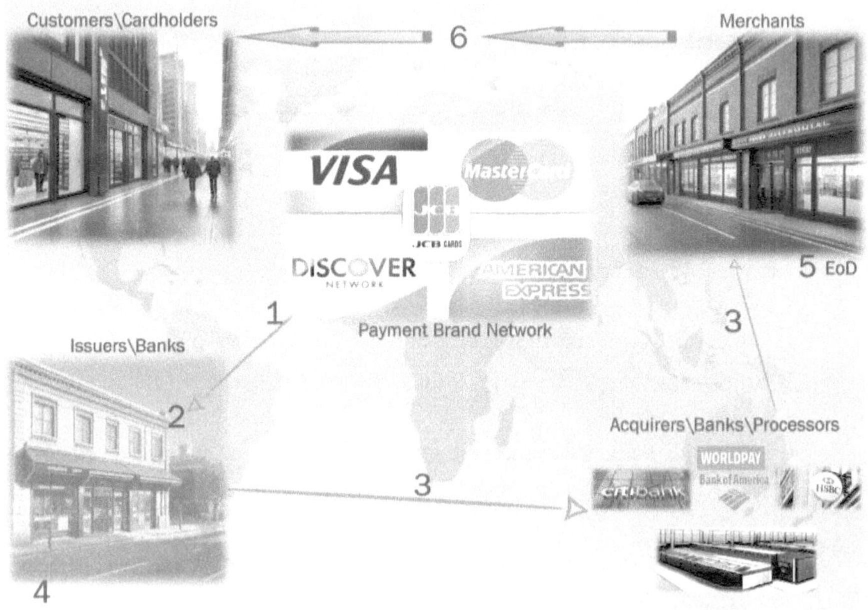

Authentication

Clearing and Settlement

1. The merchant sends a batch file of approved authorizations to the Acquiring bank or its Processor at the end of each day (EoD).

2. As part of the settlement process, the Processor routes the batched information to the Payment Brand network as a Clearing Message.

3. The payment brand forwards each approved transaction to the corresponding issuing bank.

4. The Issuing Bank will transfer the funds to the Acquiring Bank via the Payment Brand network within 24 to 48 hours of the transaction.

5. The payment Brand pays the Acquiring Bank and the Processor their respective fees from the remaining funds.

6. Cardholder purchases are then credited to the merchant's account by the Acquiring bank.

7. Once you've made purchases using your credit card, the issuing bank will send you a bill for the total amount owed. This bill will include a statement of all the transactions you made during that billing cycle. It's important to review this statement carefully to ensure accuracy and to note the due date for payment. Once you've confirmed everything is correct, it's time to pay the bill and settle your balance.

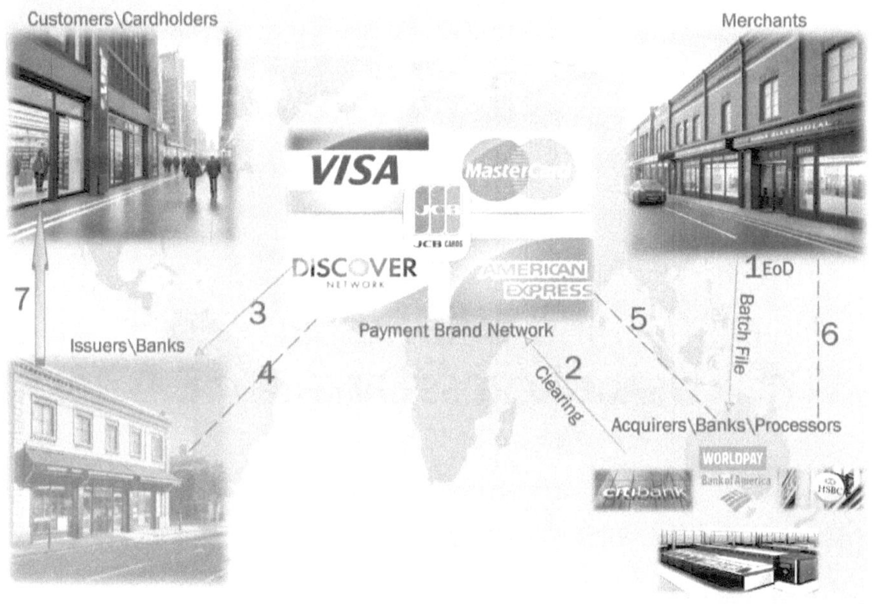

Clearing & Settlement

Tip: As far as you are concerned, Clearing is the final step, rather than Settlement.

Summary

Paying with your credit card involves several steps to ensure a smooth and secure transaction. When you present and swipe your card, a chain of authorization takes place, ultimately obtaining approval from your issuing bank. This bank then verifies your card number, CVV, customer address, and available funds to authenticate the transaction. Finally, the merchant performs batch processing, which includes Clearing and Settlement. It's important to note that this payment card ecosystem is complex. Still, by following the established process, you can trust that your credit card information is being handled safely and securely.

CHAPTER 9

UNDERSTANDING CARD SECURITY CODES AND THEIR USAGE ACROSS DIFFERENT BRANDS

Debit and credit cards are a staple in our daily lives, but have you ever wondered how they work and the security features they possess? One key security feature is the card security code, which is unique to each card and helps to protect against fraud. In this chapter, we will examine the different card security codes used by various brands. Prepare to be enthralled as I dissect the enigmatic mechanisms that safeguard your hard-earned cash, and unravel the secrets hidden beneath the surface of your flexible friend.

If you have noticed these codes, that little three- or four-digit number on the back of your debit or credit card, you will want to know the official industry terminology. It is called the Card Validation Code (CVC) or, as some like to call it, the Card Security Code (CSC).

Have you ever wondered what this code is all about? Let me tell you; it's not just some random combination of numbers and letters. This code is a crucial component in the banking system that helps ensure your money ends up where it is supposed to go. So, while it may seem like another headache-inducing detail, this code is working hard behind the scenes to make your financial transactions smoother and more secure.

The CVC is a crucial security feature that helps protect your card from online fraud. When you shop online, you don't get to swipe your card like you would at a physical store. Instead, you enter your card details into a computer system. But here's the thing: some sneaky individuals would do anything to get their hands on your card information.

That is where the CVC comes in - it adds an extra layer of protection by requiring that three-digit code to complete a transaction. This added protection helps ensure that only you (and not some cybercriminal in a dark basement somewhere) can use your card to make purchases online.

Now, I know what you're thinking. "But can't these hackers just guess my CVC code?" Well, technically, they could try. But here's the thing: most online retailers have security measures that will lock down your account after a certain number of failed attempts to enter the correct CVC. So even if someone guesses your code (which is unlikely, considering there are thousands of combinations for a three-digit code), they won't be able to use it to make purchases.

The CVC may seem just another annoying thing you must remember when making online purchases, but it's an essential tool in the fight against cybercrime. So the next time you're feeling frustrated by having to enter that three or four-digit code, remember: it's all for your protection.

The Credit Card Number

Your credit card has a unique number on the front, commonly known as the 'long number'. This number is usually 16 digits long, but in some cases, it can be up to 19 digits. It's officially called a Primary Account Number (PAN), and it's not just any ordinary number. Your credit card number is one-of-a-kind, and it contains essential details that help identify your account, card, and issuer.

The first digit indicates the provider:

- **Mastercard** numbers start with a 2 or 5.

- **Visa** card numbers begin with a 4.

- **Discover** starts with a 6.

- **JCB** begins with a 3, 2, or 1.

- **American Express** numbers start with a 3.

- **UnionPay** card numbers begin with 60 or 62.

When you use your card to make a purchase or payment, the first six digits play a crucial role in identifying the card issuer. These digits are also known as the Issue Identifier Number (IIN). The remaining numbers, excluding the last one, are specific to your account. The last digit is called a 'Check Digit,' and helps to ensure that the credit card number is accurate and in the correct order. This method of creating credit card numbers is used worldwide and was created by Hans Peter Luhn, an IBM engineer, in 1954.

Additional Security Features

The Primary Account Number (PAN) is usually found on the front of your card, but some cards have it on the back.

Your card will either show an expiration date or a valid from date. The combination is usually the month and year.

The PIN/PIN Block is the cardholder's personal identification number that you would key into a PoS device. It is not displayed on the physical card (Merchants can't store it after payment authorization)

On the back of Discover, JCB, MasterCard, and Visa payment cards, the rightmost three-digit value is the second type of card verification value or code.

On the face of American Express payment cards, the code appears as an unembossed four-digit number above the PAN, either to the right or to the left.

The code identifies each piece of plastic and ties the PAN to it.

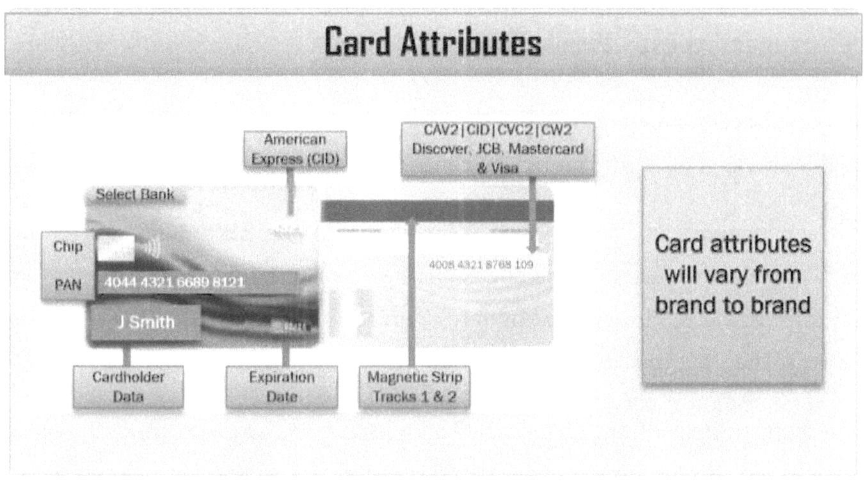

Card Security Codes by Brand

CID (Card Identification Number) - American Express and Discover payment cards - 4 digits on the front of the card

CAV2 (Card Authentication Value 2) - JCB payment cards - 3 digits on the rear of the card

CVC2 (Card Validation Code 2) - MasterCard payment cards - 3 digits on the back of the card

CVV2 (Card Verification Value 2) - Visa payment cards - 3 digits on the back of the card

CVN (Card Validation Number) – UnionPay cards – 3 digits on the back of the card

Tip: Understanding the different card security codes by brand and their locations on various payment cards is essential information for the PCIP examination.

Magnetic Stripe: Track Data

Debit and credit cards use a magnetic strip similar to a tiny strip of film. This strip is home to three tracks of payment information that are stored using magnetic fields.

The information stored on track data includes your credit card account number, name, expiration date, service code, and card verification code. Typically, credit cards only use the first two tracks. However, the third track may contain extra details like a country or currency code. Meanwhile, other magnetic stripe cards utilize all three tracks.

The magnetic strip is being phased out. This is because the magnetic stripe can become scratched or damaged in some way, resulting in the card not working. As technology advances, magnetic strips are being replaced by EMV Chips or Chip & Pin for added security and convenience.

Regarding magnetic cards used for financial transactions, there are three tracks in play - track 1, track 2, and track 3. However, you may be surprised to learn that track 3 is rarely used by major networks like Visa. It's not uncommon for this track to be absent altogether from the physical card. So when you're swiping your card at a Point of Sale terminal, it's typically reading either track 1 or track 2 (or both, just in case one of them isn't working correctly).

Track 1 data includes all fields of both tracks and can be up to 79 characters long.

The Sensitive Authentication Data (SAD), also called Full Track Data, is hidden within the magnetic strip on the back of your card.

Tip: Merchants cannot store complete track data or Sensitive Authentication Data (SAD) after authorization. Even if they use encryption or other methods to protect it, SAD cannot be retained. Under certain circumstances, the payment card brands will dictate whether issuers and processors can store SAD.

Summary

Different payment card brands have different security codes to verify transactions. American Express and Discover cards have a 4-digit CID on the front of the card, JCB cards have a 3-digit CAV2 on the back, MasterCard has a 3-digit CVC2 on the back, and Visa has a 3-digit CVV2 on the back. UnionPay has a 3-digit CVN on the back of the card. Knowing these codes and their locations is essential for the PCIP examination.

CHAPTER 10

PCI-DSS APPLICABILITY INFORMATION

To ensure secure payment card processing, merchants and service providers must comply with the Payment Card Industry Data Security Standard. This includes entities storing, processing, or transmitting sensitive authentication information besides cardholder data. So, whether you are a processor, acquirer, or issuer, it's crucial to follow these standards to ensure safe transactions.

Cardholder Data

The primary account number (PAN), when displayed, the first six and last four digits are the only digits that are allowed to be visible. The digits in between must be masked. Only personnel with legitimate business needs or requirements can see the whole PAN.

You must safeguard the cardholder name, service code, and expiration date if they are stored, processed, or transmitted with the PAN to abide by PCI-DSS and keep your sensitive information safe.

Outsourcing the Cardholder Data Environment (CDE)

If your organization outsources payment operations or the cardholder data environment (CDE) management to third parties, it's important to note that PCI-DSS requirements will still apply. The organization must ensure the account data is protected according to the strict PCI-DSS standards.

By doing so, you are taking steps to ensure the security of your customer's data and that your business remains compliant with the PCI standard.

Sensitive Authentication Data (SAD)

When you receive payment through a debit or credit card, the transaction involves Sensitive Authentication Data (SAD). This type of data helps verify the cardholder's identity and ensure the transaction's security.

SAD is a unique identifier to authenticate a cardholder and is stored on the magnetic stripe on the back of the card. It's a crucial piece of information that ensures the safety of your credit card transactions. However, if this sensitive data ends up in the wrong hands, it can make you vulnerable to fraudulent activities.

The following definitions apply to cardholder data and sensitive authentication data:

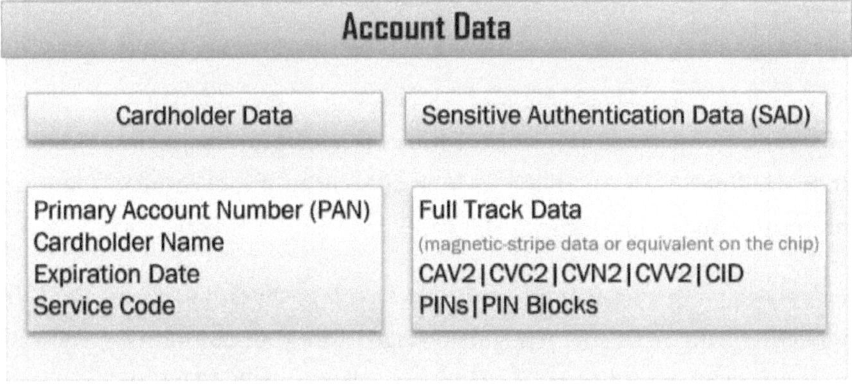

The following are the most commonly used elements of the cardholder and sensitive authentication data, along with whether they should be protected:

Account & Sensitive Authentication Data			
	Data Element	Storage Restrictions	Render Stored Data Unreadable
Cardholder Data	Primary Account Number (PAN) Cardholder Name Service Code Expiration Date	Keep Storage to a minimum: See Requirement 3.2	Yes: See Requirement 3.5 No
Sensitive Authentication Data	Full Track Data CAV2|CVC2|CVN2|CVV2|CID PIN|PIN Block	Do Not Store after Authorization: See Requirement 3.3.1	Yes. Use of strong encryption required to protect stored data until authorization completed. See Requirement 3.3.2

To comply with PCI DSS Requirement 3.5.1, only the PAN needs to be made unreadable if it's stored with other cardholder data. It's important to note that sensitive authentication data should not be stored after authorization, even if it's encrypted. Even if no Primary Account Number (PAN) is present in the environment, this rule still applies.

Tip: Storing sensitive authentication data after authorization, even if encrypted, is not allowed.

As a small business owner, you may not be aware of the importance of Sensitive Authentication Data (SAD) when it comes to credit card payments. However, understanding SAD is crucial for ensuring the security of your customers' sensitive information and complying with PCI-DSS.

Let's say you own a small online store that accepts credit card payments. If you're unfamiliar with SAD, you may unknowingly store your customers' credit card information after authorization. This is a violation of PCI-DSS and puts your customers' data at risk of being compromised by hackers.

To avoid this scenario, it's essential to understand what SAD is and how it should be protected. Sensitive authentication data includes information such as the full magnetic stripe data or the CVV2 code on the back of a credit card. This data should never be stored after authorization, as it can be used to make fraudulent purchases.

For example, let's say a hacker gains access to your online store's database and steals your customers' credit card information, including their CVV2 codes. With this information, the hacker can make unauthorized purchases using your customers' credit cards. This can lead to chargebacks, loss of revenue, and damage to your business's reputation.

By understanding SAD and complying with PCI-DSS guidelines, you can ensure that your customers' sensitive information is secure and prevent situations like the one described above. So take the necessary steps to protect your customers' data and safeguard your business from potential breaches.

Summary

To ensure secure payment card processing, merchants and service providers must comply with the Payment Card Industry Data Security Standard. This includes safeguarding cardholder data and sensitive authentication data (SAD). Outsourcing payment operations or the cardholder data environment (CDE) management to third parties does not exempt an organization from PCI-DSS requirements. Storing SAD after authorization is not allowed, but if stored can put customers' data at risk of being compromised by hackers. Protecting customers' data is crucial for avoiding chargebacks, loss of revenue, and damage to a business's reputation.

CHAPTER 11

PCI-DSS STANDARDS

If your organization needs to follow the PCI-DSS, then the PCI SSC is your go-to resource. They provide guidance, support, and top-notch training for individuals, merchants, and service providers who must comply with these standards. Plus, they offer certification and validation services to ensure you meet all the requirements. With their expertise and resources, the PCI SSC is an essential partner in helping you stay compliant with the PCI-DSS.

The PCI SSC provides several resources they are:

- PCI-DSS, P2PE, PTS (POI, HSM, and PIN).

- Card production and supporting documents.

- A Roster of QSAs, PCIPs, ASVs, and validated payment applications, PTS Devices and P2PE solutions.

- PCI Security Standards Council FAQs.

- Education & Outreach Programs.

- Participating in Organization Membership, Community Meetings, and Feedback.

Overview of the PCI-DSS Security Standards

PCI-SSF-DSS: Payment applications developed by third-party suppliers are coded securely to support PCI-DSS compliance. In a retail setting, a payment application would typically receive account data from devices such as pin entry devices, personal electronic devices, or any other connected device involved in the transaction.

PCI-P2PE: addresses the encryption, decryption, and essential management requirements for point-to-point encryption (P2PE) systems. A P2PE solution is not a requirement of the PCI SSC. However, with a P2PE solution, you can significantly reduce the scope of PCI-DSS.

PCI-PTS-POI focuses on secure pin transaction security of point-of-interaction (POI) devices and their secure components. This includes requirements such as using strong cryptography, protecting cardholder information at the point of interaction, and preventing unauthorized access to cardholder information.

PCI-PTS-PIN Security: During online or offline payment card transactions, Pin Security covers the secure management, processing, and transmission of personal identification numbers (PINs).

PCI-PTS-HSM: The purpose of this standard is in relation to the physical, logical, and device security requirements for securing Hardware Security Modules (HSMs).

PCI-Card Production: This standard covers physical and logical security requirements for systems and business processes. In particular, it is all about the requirements within a secure Card Production environment. The goal of the PCI Card Production Standard is to ensure that cardholder data is protected from unauthorized access. By following the requirements of this standard, businesses can protect their data from being stolen or compromised.

To ensure full PCI-DSS compliance, many other elements must be carefully configured and integrated into the cardholder data environment.

Think of it as building a house brick by brick. Each element must be meticulously designed and fitted together to create a secure foundation.

Only then can you have peace of mind knowing that your cardholder data environment (CDE) fully complies with PCI-DSS. So, take the time to carefully consider each requirement and ensure that your environment is built to last.

Standards In-Depth

QIR Program

Qualified Integrators and Resellers (QIRs) have been specially trained to ensure that critical security controls are addressed during the installation of merchant payment systems. By focusing on essential security controls, QIRs reduce merchant risk and mitigate the most common causes of payment data breaches by reducing merchant vulnerability.

In short, QIRs give merchants the peace of mind that their payment systems are secure. A list of QIRs can be found on the PCI Security Standards Council's website.

PCI Software Security Framework (SSF)

The PCI Software Security Framework (SSF) is a set of standards and programs that assist in developing and maintaining secure payment software. It replaces the PA-DSS and is designed with modern, flexible requirements that allow developers to incorporate payment security into their development practices without sacrificing agility or speed.

PCI P2PE

A PCI P2PE compliant solution must include encryption of cardholder data at the point of interaction (POI) or entry and secure key management of encryption and decryption devices. Validation of the solution by an independent security assessor is required. A PCI P2PE compliant solution implemented correctly, with multiple layers of protection and encryption to ensure the utmost security of cardholder data, is a true bastion of safety in an ever-evolving digital landscape. A merchant cannot access account data within the encrypted device or decryption environment, making this level of security possible.

There is no involvement on the merchant's part in the encryption or decryption operations or the management of cryptographic keys. A solution provider manages all cryptographic operations associated with a P2PE solution.

TIP: Merchants may be able to reduce their PCI-DSS scope by implementing a PCI SSC-listed P2PE solution.

PCI PTS-POI

PCI PTS-POI focuses on secure point-of-interaction (POI) devices and their secure components. The PCI PTS-POI is designed to bolster security measures at the point of interaction (POI), where customers and merchants transact. By ensuring that POI devices, such as card readers and their accompanying components, are up-to-date with the latest security protocols, the PCI PTS-POI works to safeguard customers from potential fraudulent activities. The standards set by the PCI SSC ensure that Point of Interaction (POI) devices, such as PIN-entry devices (PED), are secure. By incorporating Secure Reading and Exchange of Data (SRED) into PTS devices, the original objective of the PTS standard—protecting the PIN—is achieved. Furthermore, account data is encrypted when SRED is enabled on a PTS device. As a result, merchants can reduce their PCI-DSS scope and protect their customers' data. PCI PTS-POI is an essential component of any secure payment system.

PCI PTS (Pin Transaction Security

The PCI PTS standard was developed in response to the increasing number of attacks on payment systems. The PCI PTS standard is a crucial security measure for payment processing devices such as Point of Interaction (POI) devices, Encrypting PIN Pads (EPPs), Point of Sale (POS) devices, Hardware Security Modules (HSMs), Unattended Payment Terminals (UPTs), and non-PIN entry modules. Its purpose is to prevent theft or fraudulent use of sensitive authentication data and protect cardholder PINS and keys from unauthorized access. The Secure Read and Exchange Module (SRED) is a key component of the Point-to-Point Encryption program, which ensures that terminals are approved for secure encryption of cardholder data. To extend this security measure to non-chip and PIN cards, the PTS standard has been expanded to evaluate non-PIN entry modules against the SRED module. The PCI PTS standard complements the Payment Card Industry Data Security Standard (PCI-DSS), considered the gold standard for securing payment processing devices. From simple Encrypting PIN Pads to complex Hardware Security Modules, the PCI-DSS standard acts as a sentinel guarding the castle walls.

PCI PTS - HSM

The PCI SSC has developed the PIN Transaction Security-HSM, a standard that ensures the protection of HSMs throughout their lifecycle. PTS-HSM outlines the security requirements necessary to protect cardholder data and is evaluated to obtain device accreditation/approval. This certification covers a variety of payment processes, including PIN processing, card production/verification, ATM interchange, cash-card reloading, and key generation. PCI PTS-HSM certification requirements are primarily derived from FIPS 140-2. The thing to remember about HSMs is that they need to be PCI PTS-HSM compliant to be used in the PCI-DSS ecosystem.

Tip: The BBC has an informative program about Bank card production, the history and the technology behind them: The Secret Genius of Modern Life, Series 1, Episode 1 - Professor Hannah Fry.

PCI Card Production

PCI Card Production is a critical component of the Payment Card Industry Data Security Standard (PCI-DSS), regulating vendors that manufacture and personalize payment cards or provision payment information onto them. The PCI Card Production standard covers Logical and Physical Requirements for Card Production. It's an extensive set of controls encompassing all aspects of card production, from manufacturing and personalization to packaging and shipping. It includes logical controls covering IT assets within the High-Security Area (HSA) perimeter and physical controls extending beyond the HSA to the external environment. Card Production is a complex undertaking and requires stringent adherence to ensure a secure card production environment is always fully maintained.

Securing the card production environment requires rigorous controls, these include:

- Two people must always be present for daily processes.

- Tamper-proofing all devices with various security measures.

- A 24-hour guard room is necessary for secure card production.

- HSA walls must be built according to industry standards.

- Maintaining an accurate inventory of all assets and the location of firewalls.

Tip: The standards go into great detail when you delve into the PCI SSC documentation. Please don't panic, my experience with the PCIP 4.0 is that questions tend to be high-level rather than digging into the granular details.

Remember, if you intend to follow a career path that takes you into the payment card industry, the more you understand, the better!

Summary

As a reminder, PCI-DSS applies to all entities involved in payment card processing, including merchants, processors, acquirers, issuers, and service providers. It covers security for any system components connected to the cardholder data environment (CDE). As part of PCI-DSS, the P2PE, PTS, SSF, and PCI PIN requirements are incorporated to ensure account data is protected from the moment it is captured until it reaches the payment processor. In the Payment Card Industry, Data Security standards are an essential set of security standards designed to process and store payment card information securely. This comprehensive set of standards helps protect cardholder data from theft, fraud, and misuse. It also ensures that businesses meet the highest data security standards. Businesses must be diligent in adhering to the PCI-DSS standards to remain compliant and protect their customers' data. Compliance with the PCI-DSS standards can help companies build trust with their customers and ensure their data remains safe and secure. It's a critical component of any business's security strategy and is essential for protecting cardholder data from malicious actors.

CHAPTER 12

PCI CODE OF PROFESSIONAL RESPONSIBILITY

The PCI Code of Professional Responsibility (CPR) is the foundation of the payment card industry. It sets the standard for all Information Security Professionals involved in the payment card industry, from merchants to service providers. The CPR is a set of principles that guide individuals and organizations in their conduct and behavior when dealing with payment card data.

As a professional in the payment card industry, you must handle payment card data securely, ethically, and responsibly. The CPR outlines the expectations for professionals to ensure the safety and security of payment card data. It also provides guidance on securely and responsibly handling sensitive information, such as customer data.

By adhering to these standards, you can ensure that payment card data is secure from unauthorized access or misuse. The PCI Code of Professional Responsibility is a beacon of trust for all parties involved in the payment card industry, ensuring their data is safe.

It's important to note that all PCI SSC-qualified individuals and candidates must promote, follow, and sustain this Code of Professional Responsibility (CPR). If you intentionally or knowingly violate any principle of this Code, your qualification may be revoked, and other disciplinary action may be taken.

In short, upholding the PCI Code of Professional Responsibility is crucial for maintaining trust and security in the payment card industry.

Principles of the Code

Please note: This is only a summary of the extensive Principles, which will give you a flavor.

Being competent and exercising due care in all your work is crucial as a professional. This means being honorable, responsible, and always following the law. Ensure every aspect of your work is performed with integrity and in compliance with PCI Standards and guidance. By maintaining high standards of conduct, you'll act in the best interests of all entities you serve or support. Let's ensure we're doing our part to uphold these important values!

Only offer services you are qualified for. Keep all entities you work with promptly informed of any PCI Standards and guideline changes. Continuously learn to maintain your knowledge, skills, and experience in payment security. Promote information security standards and best practices.

Ensure that all aspects of your work are performed honorably, responsibly, and legally at all times. Maintain high standards of conduct, ensure that all PCI Standards, guidelines, and procedures are strictly followed, and provide diligent and competent service to your customers.

Violation and Enforcement

The following disciplinary measures may be taken depending on the severity of the violation:

Warning: If the situation occurs again or another violation occurs, a written warning could be issued.

Suspension: The individual's PCI SSC qualification could be suspended for all programs they participate in.

Revocation: An individual's PCI SSC qualification could be revoked for all programs in which they are actively involved.

To enforce its Code of Professional Responsibility, PCI SSC has adopted a procedure that allows fair and objective review of allegations of violations.

Tip: Memorize the Warning, Suspension and Revocation points.

In other words, as a PCIP, you must strive to uphold the highest standards of conduct, ensuring that all PCI Standards, guidelines, and procedures are always followed. Remain committed to providing the best in customer service and honorably and responsibly completing all aspects of your work to the highest legal standards. Your goal as a PCIP is to ensure every customer experience is exceptional.

Summary

The PCI Code of Professional Responsibility is a set of principles that all professionals in the payment card industry must follow to ensure that payment card data is handled securely, ethically, and responsibly. It outlines expectations for professionals to maintain high standards of conduct and comply with all PCI Standards and guidelines. The Code serves as a beacon of trust for all parties involved in the payment card industry, ensuring their data is secure. Violations of the Code may result in disciplinary action such as warnings, suspension, or revocation of PCI SSC qualification. As a PCIP, one must strive to uphold the highest standards of conduct and provide diligent and competent customer service while following all PCI Standards, guidelines, and procedures.

CHAPTER 13

SCOPING YOUR CONNECTED ENVIRONMENT

At this stage, I should mention that even though this book covers the PCI-DSS v4.0 standard, its principal aim is to provide as much information as possible to prepare you for PCIP exam day. Remember that the PCI-DSS v4.0 associated with the PCIP 4.0 exam is a complex and many-layered subject and would fill too many pages for me to cover here. However, the topics in this book, links, and references to other resources are the areas I focused on to get me over the line. With this book as your companion, you can navigate the complex and multi-faceted terrain of PCIP 4.0 like a pro.

Scoping: A Critical Step in Achieving an Accurate Understanding of the CDE

To ensure the safety of cardholder data, all components in the cardholder data environment (CDE) must adhere to the PCI-DSS security requirements. The CDE includes people, processes, and technologies that store or transmit cardholder data. These technologies come in various forms, such as network devices, servers, computing devices, and applications.

Some examples of system components include:

- Authentication servers.

- Security services.

- Internal firewalls that segment the CDE.

- Name resolution or web redirection servers that impact CDE security.

- Virtualization components like virtual machines, switches/routers, appliances, applications/desktops, and hypervisors also play a role.

Tip: Understanding what is in scope and what is not is crucial to ensure the safety and security of your cardholder data.

When thinking about your connected devices, your network, and the various payment channels, the PCI-DSS compliance landscape can seem daunting. However, PCI-DSS compliance doesn't have to be complicated. By following best practices and understanding your environment, you can ensure your devices are secure.

Before the annual assessment, assessed entities should verify that the scope of their PCI-DSS is accurate by identifying all locations and flows of cardholder data. This will help to identify all systems connected to the CDE or systems that could impact it if compromised (such as authentication servers) to ensure they are included in the scope of the PCI-DSS.

During the scoping process, it's essential to consider all types of systems and locations, including backup/recovery sites and fail-over procedures. By taking these steps, you can rest assured that you have considered all business areas.

The Scoping Process & Areas to Consider

Payment Channels – Identify all of the payment channels within your environment. This includes in-person, online, and mobile transactions. For example, imagine you run a small retail business with in-person and online payment channels. Without scoping your cardholder data environment (CDE) ahead of a PCI-DSS assessment, you may mistakenly believe that only your in-person payment terminals are in scope for compliance. However, if you fail to identify your online payment channel as also being in scope, you run the risk of non-compliance and potential financial penalties. Therefore, understanding all of the payment channels within your environment is crucial to ensuring that your business fully complies with PCI-DSS requirements.

Cardholder Data Flow – Map your cardholder data flow. This will help you understand where cardholder data is stored, how it is processed, and where it flows to.

Imagine you are a business owner who accepts online and in-store credit card payments. Before your PCI-DSS assessment, you must scope your environment and map your cardholder data flow. By doing this, you discover that your point-of-sale (POS) system stores cardholder data, but your e-commerce platform does not. You also learn that your payment gateway is transmitting data to your merchant bank but not storing it.

This information is crucial because it helps you determine which devices are in scope for the assessment. You know that you need to include your POS system in the assessment but not your e-commerce platform. It also helps you understand the flow of cardholder data and identify potential vulnerabilities or risks in the process. In this scenario, you might implement additional security measures for your POS system, such as encryption or tokenization, to better protect cardholder data.

Overall, scoping your environment and mapping your cardholder data flow is critical in ensuring that you comply with PCI-DSS and protect your customers' sensitive information.

Connected-to Systems – Identify other connected-to systems within your environment. These systems may include point-of-sale systems, payment gateways, and customer relationship management systems. By identifying all connected-to systems in your environment, you can better protect cardholder data and ensure compliance with PCI-DSS. This can also help you identify potential vulnerabilities and implement additional security measures to protect sensitive information.

Introduce Controls to Reduce the Scope – In some situations, you might be able to introduce a control that will enable a reduction of your PCI-DSS scope, thus reducing the assessment coverage. For example, if you decide to offer online ordering, your website and ordering system may also need to be assessed for compliance. However, introducing a control such as outsourcing your online ordering to a third-party payment processor can reduce your scope and simplify your compliance efforts. Knowing what devices and payment channels are in scope, and being able to introduce controls to reduce that scope, will help you save time and money in the long run.

Implement All Applicable PCI Requirements – To ensure complete compliance with the PCI-DSS 4.0 standard, you must implement all of the applicable requirements to your environment. This will ensure that you have the most secure and PCI-compliant environment possible for merchants, service providers, and financial institutions.

Maintain and Monitor Your Scope Over Time – Once you've scoped your environment and recorded your findings, maintaining the records over time is of the most importance. This will enable you to keep track of any changes made to the environment and will make the following year's assessment much easier to manage.

Perform the following steps to confirm the accuracy of the defined CDE:

- The assessed entity identifies and documents all cardholder data in its environment and verifies that no cardholder data exists outside the currently defined CDE.

- When all cardholder data locations are identified and documented, the entity uses the results to determine whether the PCI-DSS scope is appropriate (for example, a diagram or an inventory of cardholder data locations).

- Cardholder data found to be in scope of the PCI-DSS assessment is considered part of the CDE.

- Documentation that shows how the PCI-DSS scope was determined is retained for review by the assessor and for reference during the subsequent annual PCI-DSS scope confirmation.

- QSA's must validate that each PCI-DSS assessment's scope is accurately defined and documented.

Tip: A comprehensive scope of any organization's Cardholder Data Environment is one of the first steps to take and one you should remember for the PCIP.

Scoping Your Environment

I cannot overstate the importance of developing a comprehensive scope of any organization's Cardholder Data Environment. It is the foundation upon which the rest of your PCI-DSS compliance journey is built.

An adequate scope will also determine the reporting obligations for PCI-DSS, such as selecting the appropriate SAQ form or deciding whether an RoC is necessary. During the scoping task, you need to ascertain the following:

In Scope: This takes into account all payment channels, all the systems that are either directly connected to, have an impact on or are involved with the cardholder data, and the overall security of the cardholder data environment (CDE).

Out of Scope: This would mean that these systems are completely isolated and cannot interact with sensitive information. Completely cut off from any access to the CDE.

Connected to: When I talk about systems connected to the CDE, I'm referring to those not directly involved in processing a transaction and who do not store any card details. It's essential to keep this in mind to ensure the security of your sensitive information.

Assess -Evaluate the PCI-DSS requirements based on the extent of the scope.

Report - Create a comprehensive report that considers the breadth of the scope and the ultimate evaluation of the cardholder data environment (CDE).

Attest - As an entity, it is crucial always to ensure that your scope is accurate and up-to-date. When a Qualified Security Assessor (QSA) evaluates your entity, they will verify that your scope is defined correctly. So, staying on top of things and maintaining accuracy is essential to avoid potential issues.

Submit - After all the hard work, the report is finally ready to be handed over to the acquirer or a third party, such as Security Metrics.

Remediate - If the report highlights any areas needing fixing or improving, it is vital to address them promptly and in collaboration with your QSA and Acquirer. This will ensure that your business stays on track.

Tip: To easily remember the above headings, you can use the acronym SARASR: Scope, Assess, Report, Attest, Submit, Remediate

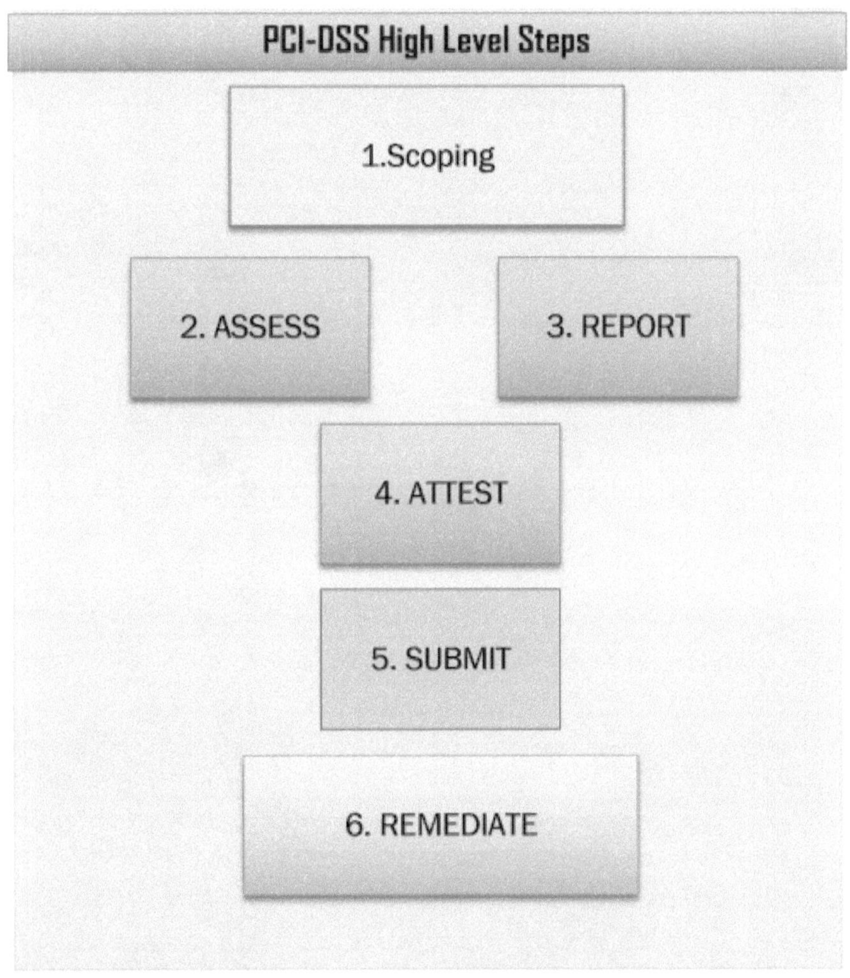

Summary

Scoping is critical in understanding the cardholder data environment (CDE) and ensuring compliance with security requirements. Before a PCI-DSS assessment, entities must verify the accuracy of their scope by identifying all locations and flows of cardholder data. Introducing controls such as outsourcing online ordering can reduce the scope and simplify compliance efforts. To confirm the accuracy of the defined CDE, the assessed entity must identify and document all cardholder data in its environment and verify that no cardholder data exists outside of it.

CHAPTER 14

CONSEQUENCES OF NON-COMPLIANCE TO PCI-DSS

PCI-DSS is not a law but an agreement, a contractual obligation between merchants, banks, and the top six payment brands: Visa Inc, MasterCard, American Express, Discover Financial Services (DFS), JCB International and UnionPay. If you don't comply with the agreement, you could face penalties ranging from a warning to a fine. The payment card brands can even ban you from accepting credit card transactions, which could lead to lost business and reduced revenue. If this happens to you, you may have to undergo a full PCI-DSS on-site audit to get back in the game. And if you're not compliant and suffer a breach, a mandatory forensic analysis may be required - which can be both time-consuming and expensive.

It's important to note that if you experience a breach of personal information, you have only 72 hours to report it to the Information Commissioners Office (ICO). Plus, credit card brands can transfer the cost of credit card replacement to you if they find that you're in breach. Imagine having to notify your customers about a security breach and then having to provide services like credit monitoring as a result - that could seriously damage your reputation!

If a case is brought against you for leaking sensitive client data, you could be held liable for any fraudulent transactions resulting from the leak. But don't let this scare you - instead, let it motivate you to implement the highest level of security protocols and procedures. As an expert in data security, it's your job to view customer data as if stored in a well-guarded vault - keeping it secure and safe from potential invaders.

When it comes to data security, always assume the worst-case scenario and take extra steps to ensure the safety of customer data. This way, you can protect your business and clients from data breaches and legal proceedings. Trust me - no one wants to be on the wrong side of a court case related to an unethical data leak.

> ***Tip: To keep the CDE secure and compliant with PCI-DSS, it's essential to regularly test your systems and applications for vulnerabilities. This should be a BAU task for your business. The actual PCI-DSS compliance submission to an Acquirer is once a year.***

To keep your business secure and compliant with PCI-DSS, you must constantly monitor your systems for any possible vulnerabilities. To ensure you're on top of things, you should include vulnerability scanning and penetration testing in your security plan. By doing this, you can spot any potential security risks and take action to protect your systems and customers from any data breaches that might happen.

But that's not all! It would help if you also had a plan in place for responding to any security breaches that do occur. That's where an incident response (IR) plan and a solid security policy come in handy. With these tools at your disposal, you can quickly and effectively respond to any potential threats and keep your business PCI-DSS compliant while safeguarding customer data from any breaches.

Summary

Non-compliance with PCI-DSS can result in penalties, fines, and even being banned from accepting credit card transactions. A breach of personal information must be reported within 72 hours, and credit card brands can transfer the cost of credit card replacement to you if you're in breach. You could also be held liable for any fraudulent transactions resulting from a leak. It's crucial to implement the highest level of security protocols and procedures to protect customer data. Compliance once a year with PCI-DSS is not enough; regular testing for vulnerabilities should be regarded as a business-as-usual task. An incident response plan and a solid security policy are also essential tools to respond quickly and effectively to any potential threats while keeping your business PCI-DSS compliant.

CHAPTER 15

MERCHANT COMPLIANCE LEVELS & REQUIREMENTS

The PCI-DSS compliance levels for merchants and service providers are categorized based on the number of card transactions processed annually. There are four merchant levels and two service provider levels.

As a PCIP, understanding the compliance level is crucial for determining the appropriate level of compliance and whether an on-site QSA audit or a self-assessment questionnaire approach is required. It also informs whether an official network scan is necessary.

Just like a treasure map, knowing the number of card transactions processed annually will lead you to the appropriate level of compliance and guide you toward the proper audit and self-assessment questionnaires.

Ascertain the annual transaction figures for a merchant from the Chief Financial Officer (CFO) or a designated finance team member.

The total number of transactions will span all payment channels, such as those taken over the counter via Pin Entry Devices (PED), automated payment devices like self-service kiosks (photo booths, supermarket quick scan checkouts, online purchases, and Mail\Telephone orders (MOTO). Be sure that the information being presented to you covers ALL transactions - don't be afraid to ask. The complete picture will give you a much more accurate picture of the merchant's compliance status.

These levels are fixed for merchants and provide an easy-to-understand compliance map.

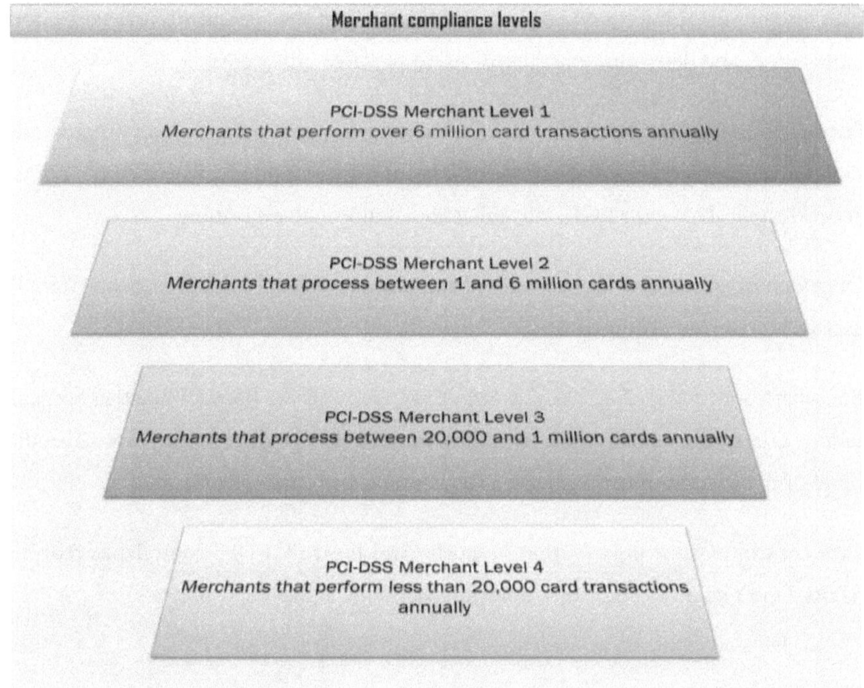

Tip: Within the Pearson VUE test environment, you can access a Whiteboard. Here you can make quick notes to help jog your memory. You will have memorized the Merchant Levels, but jotting them down on the Whiteboard will help here.

Merchant Compliance Requirements

LEVEL	QSA On-Site Review	SAQ	Report On Compliance (RoC)	Network Security Scan (ASV)
Level 1	Required Annually	N/A	Required	Required Quarterly
Level 2	Not Required	Required Annually	Requirement determined by the Card Brand	Required Quarterly
Level 3	Not Required	Required Annually	Not Required	Required Quarterly
Level 4	Not Required	Recommended (Annually)	Not Required	Recommended (Annually)

Are you aware of the critical importance of PCI-DSS compliance requirements for your organization? If you need help, let me enlighten you.

Picture this: an external assessment conducted by a Qualified Security Assessor (QSA) or Internal Security Assessor (ISA) for Level 1 organizations. The QSA will carefully evaluate your organization on-site to verify the scope of the assessment, review the documentation, and determine whether PCI-DSS requirements were met.

But wait, there's more! Not only will a QSA provide support and guidance, but they will also evaluate any compensating controls that your organization may have instead of those deemed applicable by the PCI-DSS. Talk about a thorough evaluation!

Once your organization is deemed compliant, assessors will submit a Report on Compliance (RoC) to your acquiring bank.

But what about Levels 2-4? Don't worry; they're not off the hook. While these organizations can conduct a self-assessment questionnaire (SAQ) instead of an external audit, Level 2 organizations must complete a Report on Compliance (RoC).

Take control of your organization's security and meet PCI-DSS compliance requirements. Don't let non-compliance hold you back from achieving your goals.

Summary

This chapter provided information on PCI-DSS compliance requirements for merchants and service providers. The levels of compliance are based on the number of card transactions processed annually, with four merchant levels and two service provider levels. Compliance can be determined through an external assessment by a Qualified Security Assessor (QSA) or Internal Security Assessor (ISA) for Level 1 organizations. At the same time, Levels 2-4 can conduct a self-assessment questionnaire (SAQ). It is vital to clearly understand the compliance level to determine the appropriate level of compliance and necessary audit or questionnaire approach.

CHAPTER 16

SERVICE PROVIDER COMPLIANCE LEVELS

The Payment Card Industry Data Security Standard (PCI-DSS) divides service providers into two levels according to the volume of transactions they process.

A Level One service provider will process more than 300k annual transactions, while a Level Two service provider will process less than 300k yearly transactions.

The term "service provider" refers to a business entity that is not a payment brand but is directly associated with the processing, storing, or transmitting of cardholder data on behalf of another organization.

> *Tip: A service provider is an organization that provides services that affect or may affect cardholder data security.*

Service providers deliver many services that include but are not limited to managed firewalls, IDS/IPS, Web Gateway services, and hosting services such as Infrastructure as a Service (IaaS).

Service Provider Compliance Requirements				
Service Provider Level 1	>300K Transactions/Year	Report On Compliance (RoC)	ASV Scan	Attestation of Compliance (AoC)
Service Provider Level 2	<300K Transactions/Year	SAQ	ASV Scan	

Tip: My advice is to make good use of the Whiteboard. It will free your brain up to focus on the questions! However, if you have memorized well and have a clear picture, then great!

Summary

The Payment Card Industry Data Security Standard (PCI-DSS) categorizes service providers into two levels based on the number of transactions they process per year. Level one providers process more than 300k in annual transactions, while Level two providers process less than 300k annually. Service providers are businesses that handle cardholder data security and provide services like firewalls, hosting, and web gateway services. Level one service providers require a Report on Compliance (RoC), Attestation of Compliance (AOC), and ASV Scan, while level two only requires a Self-Assessment Questionnaire (SAQ) and ASV Scan.

CHAPTER 17

CARD BRAND SERVICE PROVIDER LEVELS

As a PCIP, it is important to understand the different service levels expected from service providers by the card brands. Luckily, Mastercard, Visa, Discover, JCB, UnionPay and AMEX all provide in-depth details on their websites.

By visiting these websites and exploring the various service levels, you can better understand the levels and requirements expected from each card brand.

In addition, the card brand websites are valuable information for service providers, informing them about what they need to know about PCI Compliance.

I've listed some of the card brands and their websites below.

Mastercard Service Provider Levels

PCI-DSS Service Provider Levels | Mastercard SDP Compliant Service Providers

https://www.mastercard.us/en-us/business/overview/safety-and-security/security-recommendations/site-data-protection-PCI/service-providers-need-to-know.html

Visa Service Provider Levels

Validation of Compliance | Information Security | Visa

https://bb.visa.com/run-your-business/small-business/information-security/complianc e-validation.html

Discover Service Provider Levels

Service Provider Compliance | Discover Global Network

https://www.discoverglobalnetwork.com/solutions/pci-compliance/service-provider-co mpliance/

American Express Service Provider Levels

American Express Data Security Requirements

https://icm.aexp-static.com/content/dam/gms/en_us/optblue/us-dsr.pdf

Tip: FYI – You only need a very basic understanding of the infor-mation on these websites, so don't feel overwhelmed by the amount of content.

Summary

I've discussed the importance of understanding the different service levels expected from service providers by card brands such as Mastercard, Visa, Discover, JCB, and AMEX. I suggest visiting the respective websites to provide you with a better understanding of their levels and requirements for PCI Compliance. I've provided the links to some of the card brand's websites for further information on their service provider levels.

CHAPTER 18

APPROVED SCANNING VENDOR (ASV)

To keep your sensitive data safe from cybercriminals, you need an Approved Scanning Vendor (ASV) to scan your environment for vulnerabilities. An Approved Scanning Vendor (ASV) is a company that offers vulnerability scanning services to help organizations identify and address security weaknesses in their Cardholder Data Environment (CDE).

ASVs are certified by the Payment Card Industry (PCI) Security Standards Council, which ensures their scanning services adhere to specific standards.

ASV Responsibilities and Requirements

- Perform an External Vulnerability Scan without IDS/IPS interference, and determine if the scanned customer passed the assessment.

- Submission of the Attestation of the Scan compliance sheet.

- Avoid dangerous or disruptive testing (Scans must not intentionally alter or penetrate the customer environment).

- Provide a means for the scan customer to dispute the findings of the ASV scan.

- PCI reporting.

- Consulting with the scanned customers to determine if the IP addresses found are included in the PCI scope.

- Retain scan results for at least two years.

- Perform Host and Service Discovery and Operating System (OS) Fingerprinting.

- Take into account the presence of Load Balancers.

How do you choose an ASV?

Approved Scanning Vendors are included in the list of companies that have met the requirements set by the Payment Card Industry Security Standards Council (PCI SSC). The ASV Program is managed and overseen by the PCI SSC, which ensures that these vendors are qualified to conduct vulnerability scans on merchants' payment systems.

Tip: For internal scans of your environment an ASV is not required, but scans must be performed by qualified personnel.

Summary

An Approved Scanning Vendor (ASV) is a company certified by the Payment Card Industry (PCI) Security Standards Council to offer vulnerability scanning services to identify and address security weaknesses in an organization's Cardholder Data Environment (CDE). ASVs have specific responsibilities and requirements, such as performing external vulnerability scans without interfering with the production environment, avoiding dangerous testing and providing a means for dispute resolution. The ASV must retain scan results for at least two years. To choose an ASV, look for companies on the PCI SSC's list of qualified vendors.

CHAPTER 19

THE SIX CONTROL OBJECTIVES

PCI-DSS is one of the world's most technical and granular security frameworks and can be applied to all organizations to secure and protect their cardholder data environments (CDE). Even if you do not operate within the payment card industry, using it as a security standard will go a long way to securing your production environment.

Keep in mind adopting an industry security standard can help protect your environment, but you must decide which standard best fits your situation. Implementing the proper security measures can reduce the risk of data breaches, but equally important is implementing the measures correctly. That is why when you adhere to the PCI-DSS framework, you either comply with the controls and requirements or you do not - there is no in-between.

> *Tip: Implementing appropriate security measures can reduce the risk of a data breach, but equally important is correctly configuring those security measures. PCI-DSS uses six control objectives that work to secure the whole CDE. Each control objective has specific requirements that must be met to achieve the objective.*

For example, to protect cardholder data, you must ensure that only authorized users have access to the data and that the data is stored in a secure environment.

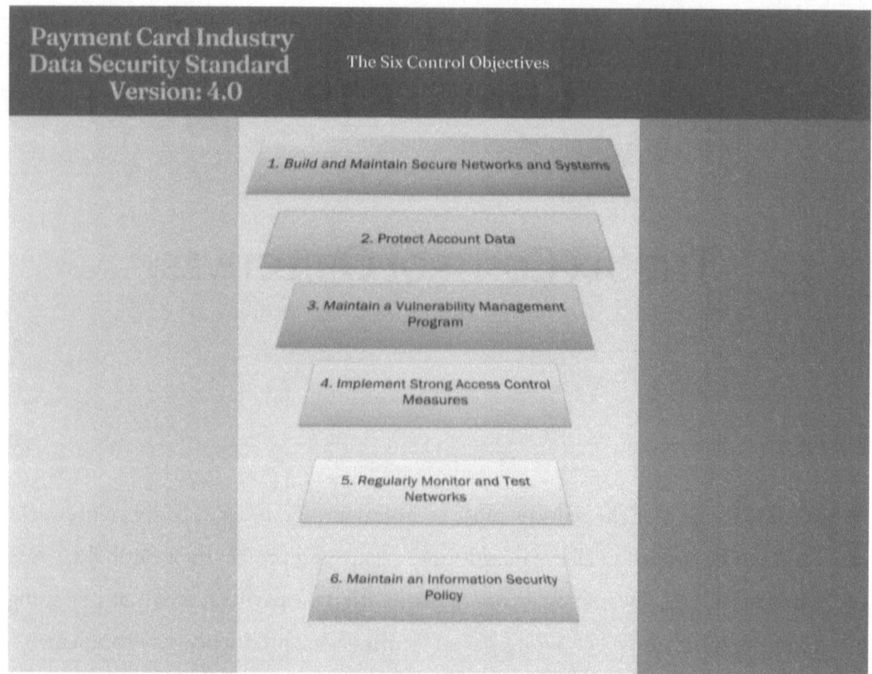

Memorize these Six Control Objectives for the PCIP exam

Tip: Memorize the Six Control Objectives for the PCIP exam.

By adhering to these control objectives, organizations can ensure that their payment cardholder data is secure and protected from malicious actors.

Within these six control objectives, there are twelve main requirements. Each of the twelve requirements has around three hundred sub-requirements or control measures.

Summary

The PCI-DSS framework is vital for securing and protecting cardholder data. Implementing the right security measures can reduce the risk of data breaches, but it is important to implement them correctly. The framework has six control objectives that organizations must adhere to ensure their payment cardholder data is secure and protected from malicious actors.

CHAPTER 20

THE 12 PCI-DSS REQUIREMENTS

As mentioned in the previous chapter, the PCI-DSS has six control objectives, and within these objectives sit twelve requirements.

Ensure you're taking the necessary steps to absorb the details and become familiar with the control objectives and the following underlying requirements.

Think of it like a puzzle - each control objective and requirement is a piece of the puzzle that you must understand how it all fits together to create a comprehensive picture of security and compliance. You can become an expert in the PCI-DSS Requirements with dedication and patience.

The Twelve Requirements

1. Install and maintain network security controls

2. Apply secure configurations to All system components

3. Protect stored account data

4. Protect cardholder data with strong cryptography during transmission over open, public networks

5. Protect all systems and networks from malicious software

6. Develop and maintain secure systems and software

7. Restrict Access to system components and cardholder data on a 'Business Need To Know basis

8. Identify users and authenticate access to system components

9. Restrict physical access to cardholder data

10. Log and monitor All access to system components and cardholder data

11. Regularly test the security of systems and networks

12. Support information security with organizational policies and programs

Tip: Memorize these 12 requirements for the PCIP exam.

PCI-DSS is an essential set of guidelines for organizations to follow to ensure the safety of their cardholder data environment. You must understand the twelve requirements, six control objectives, and the underlying security measures to pass the PCIP examination.

By taking the time to familiarize yourself with these requirements, you can ensure that you are up-to-date with these industry standards, protecting your customers' data from malicious actors and providing a secure payment environment for everyone involved.

Tip: Although the requirements are extensive, I encourage you to read them all. This will result in you being better informed and having a much deeper understanding of the requirements. So take the time to read all the requirements.

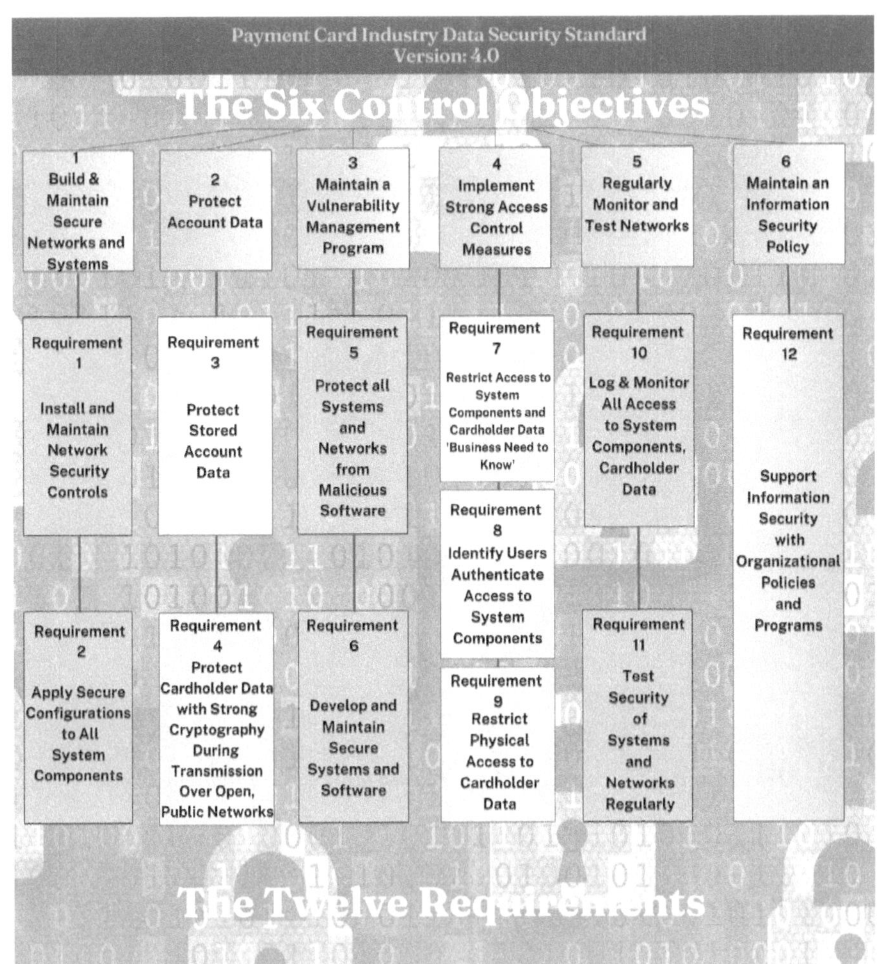

The Six Control Objectives & The Twelve Requirements

You won't be asked to list each sub-requirement by its reference number. Instead, you might come across a question that asks: **How would you comply with Requirement 9.2.1.1?**

You would then most likely be presented with a set of possible answers to choose from, such as:

a) Use Video Cameras

b) Remove Vendor Defaults

c) Encrypt Data

d) Create a Security Policy

From this example question, you can see the question refers to Requirement 9, which is about Physical Access to cardholder data. A) Use Video Cameras would be the obvious answer in this scenario.

Tip: Making tactical use of the provided Whiteboard would enable you to list the 12 Main Requirements, referring to them as needed.

Digging Deeper into the 12 Requirements

The 12 requirements are a set of granular controls that organizations must implement to meet the PCI-DSS compliance standard. Each requirement is designed to protect the security of the cardholder data environment (CDE) in a specific way.

The following section lists the control objectives (1 to 6) and an overview of their associated requirements:

Control Objective 1:

Build and Maintain Secure Networks and Systems

Requirement 1: Install and Maintain Network Security Controls is concerned with restricting network traffic via network security controls (NSCs). NSCs provide crucial protection for computer networks against potential threats from untrusted networks. These untrusted networks include the internet, wireless networks, and third-party networks beyond an entity's control. NSCs can be physical or virtual devices that enforce policies and decisions at layer 3 of the OSI model to safeguard sensitive areas, such as the cardholder data environment (CDE), from unprotected pathways. It's important to note that even if an internal network is considered trusted from an infrastructure perspective, if it's out of scope for PCI DSS assessment, it must still be treated as untrusted for PCI DSS purposes.

Organizations must install and maintain NSCs, e.g. physical or software-based firewalls, and cloud-based firewalls, also known as security groups (SG), and employ additional security measures to protect against unauthorized access to their networks and systems. Network security control rules must also be justified, regularly reviewed, and updated to reflect network and system environment changes.

NSCs are the gatekeepers of your network, ensuring only the proper traffic passes through. With a DMZ, you can create a secure buffer zone between your public and private networks, protecting sensitive data from malicious actors. NSCs should be configured with an implicit 'deny all' rule so that only explicitly allowed traffic is allowed through. By mapping out cardholder data flows, you can ensure that all data is kept safe and secure. Finally, by activating personal firewall software on all devices connected to the CDE, you can add an extra layer of protection to your network. With the right security policies and procedures in place, you can be confident that you are doing all you can to keep your data secure.

Real World Example: Imagine a scenario where you're a business owner who accepts credit card payments from customers. One day, you receive a call from a customer claiming that their credit card information was stolen after purchasing from your website. After conducting an investigation, you find out that your network was compromised and that you're responsible for the data breach. As a result, you could face hefty fines and damage to your business's reputation.

This is where requirement 1 comes in. By properly designing and maintaining network security controls, you can prevent unauthorized access to your network and protect sensitive data such as cardholder information. This means installing physical or software-based NSCs, creating a secure buffer zone between your public and private networks, and activating personal firewall software on all devices connected to the CDE.

By doing so, you can confidently assure your customers that their information is safe and secure and avoid costly data breaches. It's not just about meeting compliance standards; it's about protecting your business and customers.

Key Takeaways: In requirement 1 I talk about network security controls (NSCs) in PCI compliance. These requirements include properly designing NSCs, maintaining a data flow diagram of account data flow, justifying network traffic using the diagram, and conducting firewall rule reviews every six months to meet compliance. I emphasize the need to restrict inbound and outbound traffic to necessary communication only, block all traffic from wireless networks into the CDE, and document business justification for allowing wired or wireless traffic. I also highlight the need to restrict inbound traffic into the trusted area and list security controls for securing devices. Additionally, I mention the importance of ensuring that security controls are properly running and outline exception processes that can be leveraged as necessary.

Requirement 2: Apply Secure Configurations to ALL System Components deals with the hardening of systems and how organizations must remove vendor defaults and parameters. This includes disabling features that are not needed, such as roles and unnecessary modules on appliances, servers, desktops, laptops, and mobile devices.

The security of your organization's systems is a top priority, and the PCI-DSS ensures that every necessary measure is taken to ensure its safety. Think of it as a fortress protecting your data: you must customize its walls and locks to prevent any unauthorized access. NSCs (e.g. Firewalls) rules should be like an ever-vigilant sentry, regularly updated to ensure intruders cannot gain entry. You can keep your valuable data safe and sound with the proper steps.

By changing all system default settings, usernames, and passwords and removing any unnecessary software, you are taking proactive measures to protect your environment and CHD from potential security vulnerabilities. Additionally, encrypting all non-console access with strong cryptography and changing encryption keys when someone with knowledge leaves the organization further bolsters your security posture. Finally, documenting security policies and operational procedures will help ensure your organization complies with PCI-DSS standards.

Real World Example: Imagine a scenario where a company just launched a new software system without properly following build standards. They rushed into production without ensuring that all necessary components were in place. As a result, the system was vulnerable to hacking, leading to a data breach.

The breach occurred because the system was configured with default SNMP settings, including the use of the default community string "public." The company realized too late that it did not default to the highest security requirement when sharing functions with different security levels.

This example shows the critical importance of following build standards, properly configuring SNMP in a secure manner, and avoiding default settings to prevent potential data breaches. By adhering to these best practices, companies can avoid costly mistakes and protect their sensitive data from cyber threats.

Key Takeaways: Requirement 2 is all about ensuring we do things the right way when building a new system. This means following some essential rules and ensuring we've got everything we need before we start using the system for real. One of the most important things is ensuring different parts of the system can talk to each other securely. We need to make sure everyone who needs to use the system can access it, but we also need to ensure only the right people can see sensitive information. Another important thing is making sure we set up Simple Network Management Protocol (SNMP) in a way that keeps our data safe. This means using the latest version and not using default settings like "public" that could be easily guessed by hackers.

Control Objective 2:

Protect Account Data

Requirement 3: Protect Stored Account Data is all about how organizations must protect stored cardholder data from being accessed by unauthorized individuals. The best way to protect stored cardholder data is to take the "if you don't need it, don't store it" approach. This easy-to-follow rule can help organizations keep their cardholder data safe and secure. Think of it like a fortress - if you don't need to open the gates, keep them firmly locked! By following this simple rule, organizations can ensure that their valuable cardholder account data is not exposed to unauthorized individuals.

The security of PAN data is of utmost importance, and the PCIP expert is here to ensure it remains secure! Cryptographic keys must be securely stored using split knowledge and dual control, and all SAD must be unrecoverable. PAN data should be masked, displaying only the PAN's first six and last four digits.

> ***TIP: To ensure the complete unreadability of PAN, it is necessary to utilize keyed cryptographic hashes of the entire PAN along with appropriate key management processes and procedures. (HMAC-SHA-256 is a keyed hashing algorithm)***

All digital media, backups, and wireless network logs should be rendered unreadable. The PCIP will document security policies and operational procedures to protect cryptographic keys and ensure the safety of PAN data. Worth mentioning and remembering is that if data becomes persistent, it is crucial to ensure that all PCI-DSS requirements are met, including encryption of the stored data. This will help to protect the data from unauthorized access and ensure that it remains secure.

Masking: When displaying a PAN, only the first six and last four digits can be shown. To keep the digits in between hidden, a technique called masking is used. Masking is a way of hiding specific digits when displaying or printing the PAN. Masked PAN can potentially be unmasked.

Truncation: Truncation is a process that removes certain digits from a number and once removed, they cannot be recovered within the system. It's important to note that there's no way to undo truncation unless the PAN is recreated from another source.

By following these guidelines, entities can ensure that they comply with the latest version of the PCI-DSS 4.0 standard.

Real World Example: Protecting sensitive information such as PAN digits is crucial in today's digital age where data breaches have become commonplace. For instance, imagine a retail company that stores customer PANs without proper protection measures in place. If this data falls into the wrong hands, it could be used to make fraudulent purchases, leading to financial losses and damage to the company's reputation.

By following the requirements, organizations can ensure they have the necessary policies, procedures, and encryption methods in place to protect sensitive information and minimize the risk of data breaches. This not only safeguards the company's reputation but also helps to maintain customers' trust and confidence in the organization.

> **Key Takeaways:** Requirement 3 emphasizes the need for documented data retention and disposal policies and procedures to protect sensitive information such as PAN digits. The use of index tokens and encryption methods like disk or partition level encryption is also mentioned. Key management policies and procedures are discussed, including making strong keys, distributing them securely, and storing them securely. Key custodians have a responsibility to protect the data by protecting the keys, and service providers must provide guidance on best practices for managing shared keys.

Requirement 4: Protect Cardholder Data with Strong Cryptography During Transmission Over Open, Public Networks involves protecting data in transit, which means organizations must encrypt transmitted cardholder data when traveling across public networks. Always use strong cryptography, secure wireless networks, and restrict technologies used to transmit cardholder data to a minimum.

To ensure that your customers' CHD is transmitted safely and securely over open, public networks, such as the internet, Wi-Fi, Bluetooth, NFC and GPRS, it is essential to use a strong version of TLS, e.g.1.2 or 1.3 protocols. Never use Wired Equivalent Privacy (WEP) for Wi-Fi. Additionally, never send unprotected PAN using technologies used by end users that are not secure, such as e-mail, instant messaging, or SMS. Ensure all parties involved know the security policies and operational procedures to maintain protection for your CDE. Let's take a moment to acknowledge and keep in mind that PAN transmissions can be safeguarded by encrypting the information before it's sent, or by encrypting the channel through which the data is transmitted, or even both. Although it's not mandatory to use robust cryptography at both levels, it's strongly advised. To ensure security, it's important to keep track of all keys and certificates. Any certificates that have expired or been revoked should not be used. A self-signed certificate can be used if necessary, but only if it's been issued by an internal certificate authority (CA) within the organization.

Tip: One crucial aspect of PCI-DSS version 4.0 is the recommended use of Transport Layer Security (TLS) 1.2 or higher to encrypt sensitive data in transit. This updated version of the standard aims to enhance security measures and protect against the ever-evolving threats of cybercrime.

Real World Example: Imagine you are a customer who frequently uses their credit card to shop online. You trust that the website you are using is secure and will protect your personal information. However, without the proper precautions, your credit card information could be intercepted and stolen by hackers during the transmission process. This is where Requirement 4 of PCI DSS comes in. By following the guidelines outlined in this requirement, merchants can ensure that your personal information is protected during transmission over open public networks. This not only gives you peace of mind while shopping online, but it also helps to prevent financial loss and identity theft. So, merchants need to understand and follow the guidelines outlined in Requirement 4 to ensure the safety and security of sensitive information.

Key Takeaways: Requirement 4 is all about business owners keeping cardholder information secure. One way to do this is by sending data securely over public networks using encryption and up-to-date keys and certificates. Keep an inventory of all keys and certificates used, as different encryption methods require different key lengths. If you have a wireless network, ensure that authentication credentials aren't sent in plain text and data is encrypted using approved protocols. Use strong cryptography when sending payment account numbers outside of the normal payment process. Discard PANs that you didn't ask for. To keep your data safe from internal threats, consider using encryption for internal transmissions as well.

Control Objective 3:

Maintain a Vulnerability Management Program

Requirement 5: Protect All Systems and Networks From Malicious Software refers to protecting against all types of malware. This type of software or firmware is designed to infiltrate your computer without your consent and cause all sorts of problems for your organization. It can wreak havoc both in your business and personal life, compromising the security triad of Confidentiality, Integrity, and Availability (CIA) of your data.

Some examples of malware include adware, botnets, crypto-jacking, malvertising, polymorphic malware, and ransomware. As you are undoubtedly aware, ransomware is a particularly nasty type of malware. This is when criminals use malicious software to hold your valuable files, data, or information for ransom. It's like they're holding your digital belongings hostage! Another type of malware is called botnets. These are really versatile and can adapt quickly to try and get past your computer's defenses. They can even use other infected computers to help spread their malware! Then there's polymorphic malware, which is really sneaky. It can change its appearance to try and avoid detection, but it still does the same bad things to your computer.

It's essential to keep our computer systems and processes safe from sneaky malware that can harm our devices and steal our personal information. One way to do this is by regularly scanning for viruses or using continuous behavioral analysis. This helps us detect any hidden malware that might have slipped past our defenses. By catching it early, we can remove it and figure out how it got there in the first place.

Anti-malware solutions come in various forms, including a mix of network, host, and end-point-based controls.

This is like having knights patrolling the walls of your castle, keeping out any bad guys who might try to break in. Keeping your anti-malware software up to date is crucial to ensure it's doing its job correctly.

And finally, you should also have some anti-phishing protection in place; this must include security awareness training. Phishing is when someone tries to trick you into giving them your personal information, like your password or credit card number. An automated filter or dedicated security system can help keep you safe from these kinds of scams.

Systems considered **Not at Risk** should be identified, documented, and confirmed as not at risk by their manufacturer\vendor. Plus, continually monitored, just in case!

Stay one step ahead of malicious threats and attacks, enable Anti-malware defenses on all systems, and only disable them with full change approval, ensuring all are fully documented. Re-enable these defense mechanisms as soon as possible. Keep your defenses strong and up-to-date for the best protection.

Real World Example: The information above about the PCI DSS requirements for deploying anti-malware solutions and protecting people from phishing attacks through technical controls becomes crucial in scenarios where cybercriminals target a company's network.

For instance, a company that fails to implement proper anti-malware solutions or neglects to review and maintain them can be vulnerable to malware attacks that could compromise sensitive information such as customer data or financial records.

Similarly, not protecting people from phishing attacks can lead to employees inadvertently giving away confidential information to attackers. By following the PCI DSS requirements, companies can avoid such scenarios and maintain a secure network environment.

> **Key Takeaways:** Requirement 5 explains how you need to ensure that all your devices have proper anti-malware tools installed. You also have to perform regular checks to identify new threats and keep the anti-malware systems up-to-date. It's also crucial to keep logs of the anti-malware activities for a year and guard them against unauthorized access. Moreover,

there is a new requirement that you need to fulfill to protect yourself from phishing attacks. This calls for implementing technical defenses and automated solutions to stop these cyber attacks. And remember, this requirement applies even if you have already undergone security training. Sometimes, you may need to buy vendor products to achieve this goal.

Requirement 6: Develop and Maintain Secure Systems and Software is about having a Software Lifecycle (SLC), also known as a Software or System Development Lifecycle (SDLC) in place, or better still – a Secure Software Development Lifecycle (S-SDLC) alongside a well-maintained patch management program in operation.

An SLC and patch management program are the perfect combinations for a secure environment. They are like two sides of the same coin, working together to ensure your system remains safe and secure. With a patch management program in place, you are keeping up to date with vulnerabilities in your system, quickly identifying and patching them. The SLC provides a framework for developing secure software and systems, ensuring that any new applications or changes to existing ones are made with security in mind. These two components create a strong foundation for protecting data and meeting PCI-DSS requirements.

All (bespoke and custom) software created by or for the entity's own use, whether made specifically for them or customized from existing software, this requirement applies. Likewise, if the entity has a program that helps them with their work or a system that's been tailored to fit their needs, this requirement applies.

It is essential to patch systems regularly for known vulnerabilities and have a Software Lifecycle in place.

Additionally, having a well-documented change control process in place is essential.

Lastly, internet-facing web applications must be protected by an automated technical solution. A Web Application Firewall (WAF) would be an appropriate solution.

Tip: Pre Production was previously known as Development & Test.
Production is the live environment

Real World Example: In this digital age, keeping your information safe is more critical than ever. Unfortunately, even big companies can fall victim to data breaches if they don't practice secure design and coding. Recently, a popular online shopping site had a massive data breach because of a weakness in its code.

The developers didn't have enough training in secure coding, and they didn't review their code before putting it out there for everyone to use. This could have been avoided if they had taken security seriously and used consistent testing methods to find and fix any weak spots in their system.

All companies must prioritize security training and testing to prevent similar incidents from happening. Companies can keep their customers' information safe by making sure that only the right people can access the code on their servers. Make sure you are using different accounts for development and production.

Key Takeaways: Custom software for payment processes must meet PCI requirements and have proper security controls. Developers need training in secure design, coding practices, and security testing tools. Code must be reviewed and fixed before production, ideally with consistent validation such as Static Automated Security Testing (SAST) and\or Dynamic Automated Security Testing (DAST) as well as other forms of testing, e.g. pen testing. Processes should cover all software, including bespoke or in-house-developed software. Identified vulnerabilities must be fixed promptly and retested. Lower-risk vulnerabilities can have defined correction timeframes after budget discussions with stakeholders. The importance of restricting access to production code on application servers is highlighted, suggesting using different accounts for work in the production and development environments as a mitigation strategy.

Control Objective 4:

Implement Strong Access Control Measures

Requirement 7: Restrict Access to System Components and Cardholder Data On a 'Business Need To Know' Basis is all about administrative controls, restricting access to cardholder data on a 'business need to know' basis, and applying a Least Privilege approach to access cardholder data. By restricting access in this way, we can ensure that only those individuals with a legitimate need to access the data can do so. This will help protect the data from unauthorized access and ensure it is used responsibly.

These rules are for managing user accounts and access for anyone working with the company, whether they are employees, contractors, consultants, vendors, or third-party service providers. These rules also apply to accounts used by the company's applications and systems that use Service Accounts (SA).

Authorization controls ensure that access to cardholder data is granted only to those who need it and only when absolutely necessary. This helps create a secure environment where each user is given access tailored to their role and responsibilities, helping protect sensitive information. It's like having a key that fits the exact lock it needs to open - no more, no less.

Real World Example: Sensitive information like employee salaries and company finances is risky if accessed by unauthorized personnel. Implementing the concept of "least privilege" is a way to minimize this risk. It means employees only have access to the specific data and systems they need to do their job.

This ensures that only authorized people can see sensitive information, reducing the chance of a data breach. Regular reviews of access privileges help prevent employees from accessing sensitive data and acting as insider threats. Overall, an access control system that enforces the concept of least privilege is essential for securing sensitive data in any organization.

Key Takeaways: The concept of least privilege means giving people access only to what they need to do their jobs. To get access to special roles, higher-ups need to approve them. From time to time, the company should check things over to ensure everything's still good. The company needs to use an access control system to ensure everything stays safe. This system ensures that only the right people get into the right places. It's important to remember that just because you're you doesn't mean you're authorized to do something. The system needs to know who's who and what they're allowed to do. The company should set things up so that nobody can get in unless they've been okayed. If things don't work right, the company might have to fix them. Most companies can do everything they need to do pretty quickly. But if they have many different systems, it can be harder to keep track of everything.

Requirement 8: Identify Users and Authenticate Access to System Components covers the importance of technical access controls. Substantial password length and complexity, multi-factor authentication (MFA), no shared accounts, and accountability and traceability are like the pillars of a robust security fortress. When these measures are implemented correctly, they create an impenetrable wall of protection for the CDE.

You must implement authentication controls to ensure that only authorized personnel can access the system components. Each user has a unique user ID (not a shared or generic ID) and cannot access databases containing cardholder data directly. MFA is also used for all non-console access to the CDE for personnel with administrative access, providing an extra layer of protection.

When it comes to using a computer system, there are two important things you need to know about identifying and authenticating users. The first is ensuring we know who is using the system - this can be a person or a program. The second is verifying that the person or program is actually who they claim to be.

All Non-console (Remote Access) to the CDE for personnel with administrative access rights must be protected by **multi-factor authentication.**

Tip: Multi-factor authentication is a requirement for anyone remotely accessing the CDE from outside of the trusted network – administrators, standard users, third parties and vendors.

All **ACCESS** to the CDE must be protected by **multi-factor authentication.**

Think of it like this - when you enter a password to log into your computer or an app, you're proving that you're the person who should be using that account. This is because passwords are a common way to authenticate users. But sometimes, passwords can be hacked or stolen, which is why we use other methods like fingerprint scanners or two-factor authentication.

Overall, identifying and authenticating users is important for keeping our computer systems secure and making sure that only the right people have access to our information.

Tip: Consumer or Cardholder accounts are not governed by requirement 8

Real World Example: Let's say a company uses a remote access system to allow employees to work from home. Without proper authentication measures in place, a hacker could potentially gain access to the company's sensitive data through a compromised employee account.

By implementing multifactor authentication (MFA) for all users outside the network, the company can ensure that only authorized individuals can access the system. This is especially important for systems that could impact or gain access to the company's cardholder data environment (CDE) or related systems. Additionally, by restricting the use of interactive logins for system accounts and changing passwords periodically, the company can further protect its critical systems from potential threats.

Following Requirement 8's guidelines can help companies prevent data breaches and maintain the security of their systems and sensitive information.

Key Takeaways: Requirement 8 is all about ensuring that the right people have access to the right parts of the system. This means capturing approvals and ensuring appropriate access for every change to any part of the authentication system. It also includes sub-requirement 8.4.3, which recommends implementing MFA for all users outside the network who could potentially impact or gain access to the CDE or related systems. Even if there is no possibility of accessing or impacting the CDE, using MFA for remote access is still considered a best practice. It's crucial to identify users and authenticate access to system components, including system and application accounts. These accounts are highly privileged and need to be protected appropriately to prevent them from being compromised. Interactive logins for system accounts should ideally be blocked via technical controls. If used by a regular user, there are precise requirements around restricting use, requiring proper approval and documentation, and turning off access when work is done. It's important to note that credentials should not be hardcoded into code or config files, and passwords for system accounts should be changed periodically with appropriate complexity. By following these guidelines, you can ensure that your system components are secure and only accessible to those who need them.

Requirement 9: Restrict Physical Access to Cardholder Data takes care of physical Access. By restricting access to cardholder data only to those with a legitimate business need to know, it is much more difficult for unauthorized individuals to access this information. In addition, implementing biometric scanning, visitor procedures, controls, and restricting access to physical media, USB drives and hardcopies such as documents. All this, plus other security measures, can help further protect cardholder data.

This means employees needing access to this information to perform their job responsibilities should be granted access. However, this does not mean everyone working for your company is automatically granted access to cardholder data. First, you must determine which employees need access to cardholder data and then decide which business needs necessitate this access. Once you have defined this, you can implement appropriate access controls to ensure that only those employees with the proper authorization have access to this information.

Requirements 7, 8, and 9 aim to implement strong access control measures.

The PCIP expert ensures maximum security for cardholder data by implementing a range of physical access restrictions. Periodic inspections of PoS devices and video cameras monitoring access to sensitive areas (except public-facing areas) are all part of the security measures to have in place. It is a comprehensive defensive system that provides a fortress of protection for cardholder data, ensuring that it remains safe and secure. The security of all physical media that contain cardholder data, including both paper and digital formats, should be maintained at all times. This includes secure processes for disposing of paper records and appropriate methods for disposing of or destroying digital records.

When it comes to protecting sensitive information like credit card data, there are certain rules that need to be followed. These rules are broken down into three different categories.

Firstly, some requirements only apply to areas that are considered as sensitive areas. This means that specific security measures only need to be in place in these specific areas.

Secondly, some requirements apply to the cardholder data environment (CDE). This includes the entire CDE, as well as any sensitive areas that are within it.

Lastly, some requirements apply to the facility as a whole. These controls are in place at the physical boundary of the business premises, such as a building, office area, or perimeter. They exist outside of the CDE and sensitive areas, and may include things like a guard desk that checks the identification of visitors.

Real World Example: Imagine a scenario where a retail store experiences a data breach due to a compromised point of interaction (POI) device. The store did not implement proper controls, such as regularly inspecting and inventorying their POI devices, and did not train their personnel to identify compromised devices. As a result, the store's customers' cardholder data was stolen, leading to a loss of trust and reputation for the store and potential legal and financial consequences.

This real-world example highlights the importance of implementing PCI-DSS controls to protect cardholder data and prevent breaches. By following industry standards and implementing proper controls, organizations can ensure the security of their customers' sensitive information and avoid potentially devastating consequences.

Key Takeaways: The requirement emphasizes the importance of physical security in protecting cardholder data. It highlights that technical controls alone are insufficient to prevent malicious actors from accessing sensitive information if physical security measures are lacking. The requirement also mentions specific conditions, such as not providing easy access to network jacks and securing wireless devices, to ensure compliance with industry standards. PCI controls focus on protecting cardholder data, including ensuring it is stored securely and logged appropriately. Sub-controls include storing data in a physically secure location or using a tape management organization to collect and store media. It is also important to keep track of which media has been sent and where it has gone. The requirement outlines the importance of protecting physical payment devices as part of PCI-DSS. Point of interaction (POI) devices, such as card readers, must be inventoried and inspected regularly, and personnel should be trained to identify compromised devices. The training outlined in 9.5.1.3 puts a lot of responsibility onto the personnel nearest these systems. The sub-controls to 9.5.1 state that you have to know the makes, models, locations, and serial numbers of all your devices to validate that the ones you're using to take payments are the right ones.

Control Objective 5:

Test and Monitor All Network Systems

Requirement 10: Log and Monitor All Access to System Components and Cardholder Data should be a primary task for any organization and must be part of its day-to-day security activities.

PCI-DSS requirement 10 outlines the complex process of collecting and monitoring logs from all devices covered by the standard. It is necessary to store all of these audit logs and analyze them for security events and other suspicious activity.

Automated Reviews of logs are required (10.4.1.1) – see the note below-regarding applicability timelines.

Whenever an alert is received, it should be followed up on and partnered with an incident response process that is ready to take action if necessary.

The cardholder data environment requires an extra layer of security to ensure that all access to systems and data is tracked and monitored. The audit logs generated by these systems provide a tamper-proof record of activities, allowing for alerts, tracking, and analysis. Time synchronization across all systems ensures that the data is consistent and makes it easier to analyze logs across multiple systems. With this system, organizations can be confident that their cardholder data is always secure and monitored.

Note: Requirement 10 does not apply to consumers or cardholder activity.

Real World Example: The information above about PCI DSS Requirement 10 would be helpful for any organization that handles payment card data. For example, let's say a retail store experiences a security breach where the payment card data of their customers is compromised. The store would need to investigate the breach and identify the cause.

With the knowledge of Requirement 10, the store would know that they need to check their critical security control systems such as network security controls, file integrity monitoring, physical access controls, and segmentation controls if used. They would also need to ensure that their logs have accurate timestamps and review them periodically to detect any anomalies. If any failures are detected, they need to address them and document the failure and recovery process promptly.

By following these requirements, the store would be able to restore security, take necessary actions, and prevent similar breaches from happening. Therefore, understanding and implementing Requirement 10 of PCI DSS can help organizations protect their customers' payment card data and avoid costly security breaches.

> **Key Takeaways:** To keep things running smoothly, organizations need to keep their clocks synchronized. That's where the Network Time Protocol (NTP) comes in. But it's not just a matter of setting the clock and forgetting about it - some strict controls need to be followed, as outlined in requirement 10.6.2. This includes having a formal time server and restricting access to time settings. Of course, it's not just about keeping the clocks in sync - there's also the matter of keeping an eye on things to ensure nothing fishy is going on. Automated log reviews are allowed under requirement 10.4.1.1, while periodic reviews of system components are mandatory under requirement 10.4.2. These reviews help identify any unusual activity that could indicate a security breach. But what happens if a breach does occur? Service providers need to be on the ball, quickly detecting, alerting, and fixing any system failures as per requirement 10.7.2. This is mandatory for all organizations until March 2025, after which it becomes a requirement for service providers only. And if a breach does occur, requirement 10.7.3 outlines the necessary steps that must be taken, including restoring security, documenting the recovery process, taking required actions, and restarting monitoring if it was stopped.

Requirement 11: Testing Security of Systems and Networks Regularly are resource intensive and will take considerable planning and a significant amount of an organization's budget to pay for an Automated Security Vendor (ASV). However, vulnerability scans, penetration testing, and the resultant remediation tasks ensure that all in-scope systems and applications remain secure from one day to the next.

The importance of Requirement 11 cannot be overstated. With proper planning and budgeting, Requirement 11 can be a powerful tool for keeping your organization's data safe and secure.

As a PCIP, ensuring the security of your systems and processes is essential. Regular penetration testing should be conducted to understand the CDE and critical systems in-depth. Additionally, intrusion detection and prevention systems (IDS/IPS) should be employed at the perimeter of the CDE and other critical points. Vulnerability scans should also be performed regularly, as well as when there are significant changes to the environment. A change detection/file integration management (FIM) system should be used to detect and manage unplanned changes to system-critical files. Finally, ensuring that no unknown/unwanted/rogue wireless access points are present on the network is crucial.

Tip: The customized approach is not applicable to requirement 11.

Real World Example: As an online business owner, ensuring the safety of your customers' credit card information is paramount. And that's where the PCI DSS comes in. These security requirements are crucial in safeguarding your customers' data, and one of them is about scanning for vulnerabilities.

Regularly scanning your website for vulnerabilities, especially after significant changes, is imperative. Monthly scans can help you detect and fix any issues promptly. In case anyone asks, keeping track of how you conduct these scans is also essential. And if you hire someone to help you out, ensure that they retest everything after you've made the necessary fixes. PCI DSS also mandates that you have systems in place to detect intruders and any changes to your files. This way, you can take swift action if required.

If you run an e-commerce business, you must be extra vigilant regarding payment pages. Adhering to these requirements may mean spending some extra cash, but it's a small price to pay to keep your customers' information safe.

Key Takeaways: To keep your organization's network secure, you need to comply with requirements set by the Payment Card Industry Data Security Standards (PCI DSS). One of these requirements is to conduct internal vulnerability scans after any significant changes, regardless of the regular three-month scan cycle. If you decide to conduct a penetration test using your own team, ensure they are qualified and independent and document their process for meeting the methodology. If you hire a third-party provider, ensure that they will retest to confirm that any issues have been fixed. Another requirement is to have intrusion detection and prevention systems in place, with alerts configured and software kept up-to-date. Service providers also need to detect covert malware communication channels. Critical files should be checked weekly using change-detection tools, and any unauthorized changes should be handled appropriately. E-commerce merchants must have a detection mechanism in place for unauthorized changes on payment pages, checked at least once every seven days or more frequently based on targeted risk analysis. These new controls may require budget discussions to ensure compliance with PCI DSS requirements.

Control Objective 6:

Maintain a Security Policy

Requirement 12: Support Information Security with Organizational Policies and Programs covers all policy and procedure documentation, annual risk assessments, security awareness training, incident response plans, and third-party due diligence.

Finally, PCI-DSS requirement 12 is designed to ensure the highest level of security for all personnel. It is an impressive example of how the PCI-DSS standard is intended to protect companies and their customers from cyber threats.

Organizations must prioritize information security to ensure their data is protected. To accomplish this, a comprehensive security policy should be established, regularly updated, and rigorously enforced. Additionally, a robust incident response plan should be developed and tested periodically to ensure its effectiveness. Third-party managed service providers (MSPs) must also be carefully managed and monitored to ensure their compliance with security policies. Furthermore, employees should be thoroughly screened before hiring, and individuals should be assigned key security tasks. Finally, policies for the use of critical technologies should be implemented. By taking these steps, organizations can create a secure environment for their data and protect it from potential threats.

Real World Example: Imagine a scenario where a small business owner uses a third-party payment processor to handle their customers' credit card payments. The payment processor experiences a security breach, resulting in the theft of sensitive customer data. The small business owner is now liable for the damages caused by the breach, including potential fines and lawsuits.

This is where the information outlined in Requirement 12 becomes crucial. By following the policy and procedure documentation, conducting annual risk assessments, and implementing security awareness training and incident response plans, the small business owner could have taken steps to mitigate the risk of a breach and minimize the damage in case of one. Moreover, by performing ongoing due diligence of the payment processor and ensuring they meet the PCI DSS compliance requirements, the small business owner could have avoided partnering with a payment processor that is not fully secure.

> **Key Takeaways:** Requirement 12 is all about keeping your information safe with policies and programs. This includes things like making sure everyone knows how to stay safe online, having a plan for when things go wrong, and checking that other companies you work with are also following the rules. If you work with other companies to process payments, they need to show that they are following the rules too. They have to write down what they do to keep things safe and fix any problems they find. Starting in March 2025, everyone will also have to learn more about how to stay safe when working with other companies. Before you start working with a new payment company, you need to ensure they follow the rules too. It's essential to check that everything stays safe even if it's on a computer that's not really there. You also need to ensure the payment company is scanning for problems and fixing them. Finally, the payment company has to give you the information you need to stay safe too.

> *Tip: At the end of each requirement, there is always a sub-requirement addressing policy documentation.*

A complete list of the 12 Requirements and their 300+ Sub Requirements can be viewed in the PCI DSS v4.0-March.2022 document on the PCI-SSC website (Page 39 onwards). Follow: https://www.pcisecuritystandards.org/document_library/ and look under the heading of Standard.

To understand what each requirement is about, reading the overview at the beginning of each requirement in the official document is worthwhile.

Important: Please ensure that you read each of the requirements in the official document in their entirety.

Special Note: Just a quick heads up - some **new additional sub-requirements** are included within the 12 requirements. These will only be treated as best practice until March 31, 2025 when PCI-DSS v4.0 becomes the only standard to follow and at that point all requirements become mandatory.

If you're interested in learning about the new PCI-DSS changes, you can check out the **PCI DSS Summary of Changes** document on the PCI SSC website. Just head over to https://www.pcisecuritystandards.org/document_library/ and take a look.

Once you're there, skip to page 28 and find the section called **Summary of New Requirements**. It's all explained there in a clear and friendly way that's easy to understand.

CHAPTER 21

COMPENSATING CONTROLS

Compensating controls are used when the original requirement can't be implemented due to technical or business constraints. But keep in mind – they have to be just as rigorous and offer the same level of protection. Compensating controls are like a trusty sidekick that helps you achieve your requirement goal while offsetting any risks that may come your way.

> *TIP: Remember that a compensating control is a type of internal control that is used to reduce the risk when a PCI-DSS requirement can't be met. However, the compensating control must adhere to the same intent and rigor as the original PCI-DSS requirement.*

A Valid Compensating Control Must Adhere to the Following Four Points:

1. To ensure compliance with the PCI DSS requirement, meeting the original standard's intent and rigor is essential. This means going beyond mere surface-level adherence and genuinely understanding the underlying principles and objectives of the requirement.

2. Provide a similar level of defense as the original PCI DSS requirement while also ensuring that all necessary security measures are in place to protect against potential threats and vulnerabilities.

3. Strive to go "above and beyond" the original PCI DSS requirement by implementing additional security measures and controls that go beyond the minimum standards.

4. Make sure that the level of risk you are taking by not following the PCI DSS requirement is proportional to the potential benefits or gains you might get.

What Is Regarded as a Valid Technical or Business Constraint?

Remember, you can't just use a compensating control because you don't feel like following the original requirement. That's not a valid reason! To be considered valid, you must have a legitimate technological or documented business constraint preventing you from using the original requirement. And before you implement a compensating control, ensure you've conducted a risk assessment.

To ensure that your compensating control is up to standard, it must first be reviewed by a QSA. Think of them as the wise old sage who gives their blessing before you embark on your quest. So, if you want to go above and beyond the PCI-DSS requirements and become a true hero in the world of internal controls, make sure you're using compensating controls for all the right reasons.

Valid Documented Business Constraint

Let's say you run a small online business that sells handmade jewelry.

You've been following the PCI-DSS requirement to encrypt all credit card information stored on your website. However, due to limited resources, you cannot invest in high-end encryption software that meets the PCI-DSS standards.

In this case, a valid business constraint would be the lack of **financial resources** to purchase the required encryption software.

- A potential compensating control could be to use a third-party payment processor that handles encryption and PCI DSS compliance on their behalf.

Legitimate Technological Constraint

Let's say you work for a company that processes credit card payments. One of the PCI-DSS requirements is to use multi-factor authentication for all remote access to the company's network. However, due to the nature of your company's legacy software, it cannot support multi-factor authentication. In this case, a valid technical constraint would be **the inability of the legacy software to support multi-factor authentication.**

- A possible compensating control could be implementing a VPN with strong encryption for remote access, combined with strict access controls and monitoring.

Please remember these are examples only

Summary

To be clear, compensating controls can be used to reduce the risks associated with specific requirements, but only if they meet the same level of rigor and intent. Plus, they must provide a similar level of protection while offsetting risks the original requirement was designed to mitigate. Just keep in mind that for compensating controls to be valid, they must be reviewed by a PCI QSA. And don't think you can use them because you disagree with a PCI-DSS requirement. Compensating controls should only be used when a valid technical or business constraint prevents you from adhering to the original requirement.

CHAPTER 22

THE APPENDIX

Appendixes apply to different types of entities and are in addition to the PCI-DSS Requirements.

They provide additional requirements tailored to different entities, allowing you to build a secure and compliant customer environment. With the right combination of PCI-DSS Requirements and Appendix, you can create a fortress of security for your customer's data.

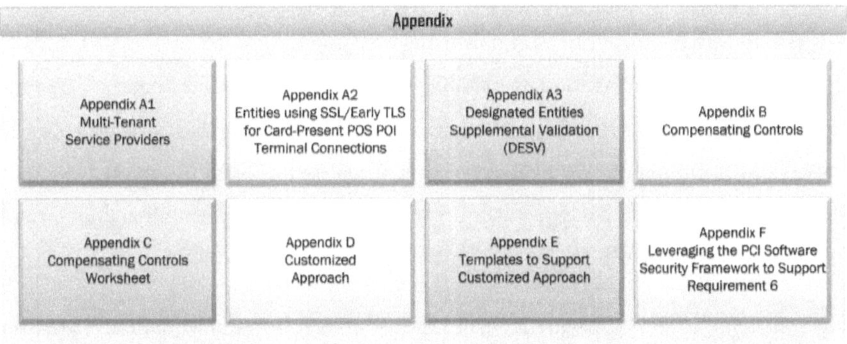

Tip: As well as reading and understanding what each of the appendixes is for, it will serve you well to memorize the appendix headings as in the diagram above.

Appendix A1: Additional PCI-DSS Requirements for Multi-Tenant Service Providers (Shared Hosting Providers)

The PCI-DSS Appendix A is designed for multi-tenant or shared hosting providers who wish to provide PCI-DSS-compliant hosting to their merchant and/or service provider customers. The PCI-DSS Appendix A is a powerful tool that multi-tenant or shared hosting providers can use to ensure their merchant and/or service provider customers can safely conduct transactions in a PCI-DSS-compliant environment. By leveraging this resource, providers can ensure their customers are safeguarded against any potential data breaches or other security issues. Appendix A is a crucial resource for any shared hosting provider looking to offer their customers the highest level of protection and compliance.

Appendix A2: Additional PCI-DSS Requirements for Entities using SSL/Early TLS for Card-Present POS POI Terminal Connections

It is essential that POS POI terminals using SSL and early TLS upgrade to a strong cryptographic protocol as soon as possible. Furthermore, SSL and/or early TLS must not be introduced into environments that do not already support those protocols. The known vulnerabilities in POS POI payment terminals are difficult to exploit at the time of publication. As a result, it is up to the organization to keep up with vulnerability trends and determine whether their devices are susceptible to known exploits.

The security of POS POI payment terminals is of utmost importance, and organizations must stay ahead of the curve to protect their customers. Keep your customers' data safe by upgrading to a robust cryptographic protocol and avoid using SSL and/or early TLS in unsupported environments. This is a crucial step in protecting your customers from any known vulnerabilities. It's like building a fortress around your customers' data - the more robust the walls, the better protected they will be!

Appendix A3: Designated Entities Supplemental Validation (DESV)

Appendix A3 applies only to entities designated by a payment brand or acquirer as needing additional validation of PCI-DSS requirements. This Appendix may apply to the following entities:

Those who store, process, and/or transmit large amounts of cardholder information. Providers of data aggregation points for cardholder data. Those subjected to significant or repeated breaches of cardholder data in the past. By validating business-as-usual (BAU) processes and increasing validation and scoping considerations, these supplemental validation steps are intended to increase the assurance that PCI-DSS controls are maintained effectively and continuously.

As a PCIP expert, you must understand that it is essential to maintain adequate and continuous controls to protect cardholder data. Implement additional validation steps for those who store, process, and/or transmit large amounts of cardholder data and providers of data aggregation points. This will ensure that any entities that have suffered past cardholder data breaches will be better protected in the future, meaning data breaches are avoided and business-as-usual processes are validated.

Appendix B: Compensating Controls

When an entity cannot meet a requirement explicitly due to technical or business constraints, compensating controls can be implemented to mitigate the associated risk. These controls allow organizations to continue protecting their customers' data while meeting the PCI-DSS requirements.

For compensating controls to be effective, they must meet the following criteria:

In terms of their intent and rigor, they must meet the original PCI-DSS requirements. Using compensating controls, it should be possible to provide a similar level of defense to that offered by the original PCI-DSS requirement, so that the compensating controls are sufficient to mitigate the risk. You must go "above and beyond" any other PCI-DSS requirements that you must comply with. Compliance with other PCI-DSS requirements is not a compensating control.

Compensating controls are a powerful tool for ensuring PCI-DSS compliance. They provide an alternative to the original PCI-DSS requirements, allowing organizations to achieve the same level of data protection while meeting their unique security needs. By assessing their risk profile and implementing appropriate compensating controls, organizations can ensure their data is secure and their customer's information is kept safe.

Appendix C: Compensating Controls Worksheet

PCI SSC provides organizations with a worksheet for documenting and defining compensating controls.

The compensating controls worksheet contains the following areas that require completing:

- Constraints

- Definition of compensating controls

- Objective

- Identified Risk

- Validation of Compensating Controls

- Maintenance

Appendix D: Customized Approach

This appendix is for organizations that want to meet a specific PCI DSS requirement but not in the exact way it is defined. It allows them to come up with their own strategy to meet a requirement's objective while designing security controls that are unique to their organization. Say goodbye to a one-size-fits-all approach and hello to a customized strategy that meets the specific requirements of an existing, mature security posture.

What Is the Defined Approach

The defined approach requirement is about following the guidance set down by the PCI-DSS 4.0 framework to meet a requirement and, in reality, is no different from the guidance that was in the previous PCI-DSS version 3.2.1 standard. However, where an entity has a valid business or technical constraint that prevents them from following the defined approach, then and only then can they introduce a compensating control to meet the requirement.

The Customized Approach

The customized approach is all about designing security controls specific to your organization's needs. It allows you to tailor your security measures to your unique circumstances, ensuring that you meet the objectives of a specific PCI DSS requirement in a way that makes sense for your business. This approach gives you the freedom to create a customized strategy that fits your organization's individual needs, while still meeting the overall goal of the requirement. It's a flexible and effective way to take ownership of your security measures and ensure they are up to par. However, extra documentation is required and must be maintained to evidence each customized control. Targeted risk analysis (TRA) must be performed for each customized control. Entities following the customized approach aren't permitted to use any compensating controls.

Tip: It's crucial to maintain assessor independence, which means that if an assessor has created a customized control, implemented it, completed the controls matrix, or conducted a TRA, then another assessor must perform the actual assessment. This en-

sures fairness and impartiality in the assessment process and con-
tributes to maintaining the highest standards of quality.

In practice

An internal security assessor (ISA) might perform the TRA and test the implementation of the contol. Once this is done, a qualified security assessor (QSA) can step in and conduct their own assessment. This ensures that all bases are covered and the control is thoroughly evaluated.

Entity Responsibilities

To ensure the effectiveness of customized controls, it is important to maintain evidence and complete the Targeted Risk Analysis Template in Appendix E2. All information should be documented in the Controls Matrix template.

Assessor Responsibilities

Verifying whether an entity meets all Customized Approach documentation, deriving testing procedures for each customized control, and determining whether the control meets the Customized Approach objective.

◈

Appendix E: Templates to Support a Customized Approach

This appendix contains some handy templates for you to use as a guide when documenting your organization's control matrix and targeted risk analysis. Please note these templates are just examples, so in practice, you could use a different format if you prefer. However, ensure you include all the information outlined in these templates, no matter your chosen format.

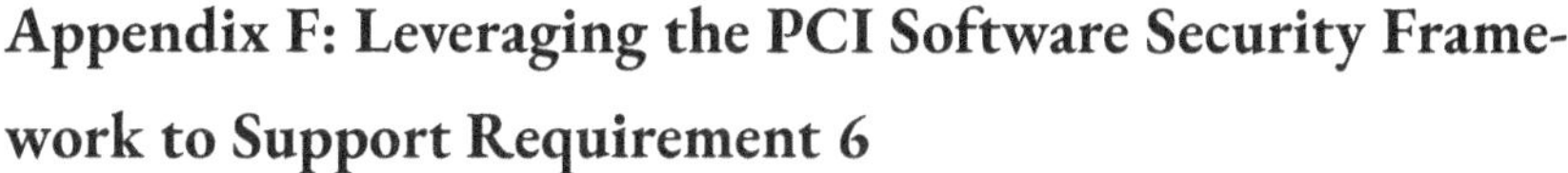

Appendix F: Leveraging the PCI Software Security Framework to Support Requirement 6

To meet the secure systems and software requirements in PCI DSS Requirement 6, Merchants and Organizations can use custom software that follows the PCI SSC Secure Software Standard and Secure SLC Standard. This saves time and effort as additional testing is not required. It may also help meet other requirements through the Customized Approach.

Summary

The PCI-DSS has several appendices that provide additional requirements for multi-tenant service providers, entities using SSL/early TLS for card-present POS POI terminal connections, designated entities requiring supplemental validation, and organizations wanting to meet specific PCI DSS requirements in a customized way. The compensating controls worksheet includes areas such as constraints, definition of compensating controls, identified risks, and validation of compensating controls. Appendix F outlines how merchants and organizations can use custom software that follows the PCI SSC Secure Software Standard and Secure SLC Standard to meet secure systems and software requirements.

CHAPTER 23

SELF ASSESSMENT QUESTIONNAIRES (SAQ'S)

What are SAQs?

At a basic level, they are a set of questionnaires or validation tools intended to assist merchants and service providers in self-evaluating their compliance with the PCI-DSS. There are eight SAQs, labeled SAQ-A through to SAQ-D for Merchants. For Service Providers, there is a separate SAQ-D.

The PCI-DSS Self-Assessment Questionnaires (SAQs) are the navigational map that merchants and service providers need to chart their way to compliance with the PCI-DSS. With its helpful guidelines, the SAQ is the lighthouse that leads companies safely to shore, ensuring they don't get lost in the choppy waters of data security.

Merchants and service providers must always comply with the PCI-DSS as applicable to their environments. That means that an organization must always remain compliant beyond the date of attestation.

If you suffer a breach and the forensic investigators are called in, they will be interested to know if you were compliant at the time of the breach. It won't matter if you start waving your PCI-DSS accreditation in their face, dated six months ago! No, it's whether you have maintained your PCI-DSS compliance throughout.

In other words, PCI-DSS Compliance is not a one-time event - it is an ongoing process! It must be part of your business-as-usual (BAU) day-to-day operation.

The PCI-DSS is like a vigilant sentry, always on guard and ready to protect your cardholder environment from cyber threats. But, like any sentry, it must be constantly maintained and updated to remain effective.

- Please note that an SAQ that only covers some PCI-DSS requirements applicable to your environment may indicate that an alternative SAQ may be more suitable for your environment.

- To be PCI-DSS compliant, you must also comply with all applicable requirements.

TIP: To be eligible for any of the SAQ's, apart from SAQ D, there must be no electronic storage of cardholder data (CHD).

Tip: To tackle SAQ related exam questions, it's necessary to memorize each SAQ and understand its applicability. Being able to recall the SAQ's at will is crucial.

Eligibility Criteria for Self-Assessment Questionnaires

SAQ(A)

- SAQ(A) Card-not-present (e-Commerce or mail/telephone (MOTO) order merchants.

- All Cardholder data functions are outsourced.

- SAQ(A) does not apply to face-to-face merchants.

- This SAQ asks 20+ individual questions; some may be regarded as not applicable; however, if a merchant answers not applicable, then a full explanation must be given as to why it doesn't apply to their environment.

- The SAQ A applies where the merchant website is fully hosted by a PCI-DSS-validated third-party service provider responsible for all data security and privacy aspects.

- Customers are redirected from the merchant's website to a PCI-compliant, third-party payment processor, where no elements of the page originate from the merchant's site. **The use of an iframe or URL usually provides the redirect.**

Tip: The responsibility for compliance sits with the merchant. What do I mean? So, even though the organization has outsourced its entire card data processing, the data is stored with a third-party provider. PCI-DSS states that the responsibility sits with the merchant. Remember that you must verify that your third parties do not present a threat and that this fact has been validated.

SAQ (A-EP)

- SAQ (A-EP) This SAQ is designed for e-Commerce merchants only, who partially outsource their payment processing, but not the administration of the websites that link to it and therefore require proper protection if they are to remain in business.

- The merchant carries out the administration of an SAQ A-EP environment. What does this mean? The merchant's website creates a payment form, along with the payment data, which is posted directly to a PCI-compliant third-party payment processor.

- Alternatively, the merchant's website redirects consumers to a PCI-compliant, third-party payment processor. However, some elements of the payment page come from the merchant's website.

- The third-party service provider's (TPSP) PCI-Compliance must be formally proven for the services provided. This can be achieved by reviewing the TPSP's Attestation of Compliance (AoC).

- This SAQ requires merchants to answer 190+ questions, explaining any questions they do not think apply to their environment.

- The benefit of a merchant looking after the administration of the payment form is that these forms are highly configurable; branding can be incorporated, making them feel like the cardholder or customer has a more streamlined shopping experience. The downside is that the merchant's website is a target for hackers.

As an expert in security, I can confidently assert that protecting the webserver that links to the payment processing system is essential to ensure the success of any e-Commerce business. Without proper security measures, the company is at risk of data breaches, fraud, and other malicious activities that can harm its operations.

Consider actively monitoring for changes and implementing a Web Application Firewall (WAF). Hackers will attempt to introduce malicious code into your website to steal data or inject illegitimate ads. A WAF can help detect and prevent these attacks. Monitoring for or preventing changes will prevent hackers from capturing payment card details before redirecting the cardholder (customer) to the service provider.

SAQ (B)

- SAQ (B) This SAQ only applies to mail\telephone orders (MOTO) or face-to-face transactions; it can't be used for eCommerce transactions.

- A merchant is required to respond to just over 40 questions, with explanations for any questions that do not apply to their environment.

- The SAQ B should be completed by merchants who only process payment card data using imprint machines or standalone dial-out terminals as the payment method.

You will most likely never see imprint machines associated with SAQ B again. I've used these things in the past, in the 1980s and into the millennium. At that time, I was particularly concerned about the merchant's storage of the carbon receipt, as they could be lost in transit or copied by staff.

These old imprint machines used a layered set of rectangular carbon and receipt papers. The credit card was placed face-up on the device, with the carbon receipt paper on top. A roller was then pulled across by hand. Often you would scrape your knuckles on the machine, hence the name 'Knuckle Busters.'

- Standalone dial-out terminals accept Chip & PIN, swipe cards, or manually keyed transactions.

- To qualify for SAQ B, the dial-out terminal must only be connected to a telephone line.

Merchants using standalone dial-out terminals and Knuckle Busters (if they still exist) must pay attention to their physical security environment. That means limiting access to areas of the organization that store sensitive data. Merchants must take the necessary steps to protect their data and secure their systems.

SAQ (B-IP)

- SAQ (B-IP) is designed for merchants who do not store cardholder data (CHD) in digital format, and only use IP-based, Chip & PIN point-of-interaction devices (POIs).

- It should be noted that these merchants can handle both card-present (brick-and-mortar) and card-not-present (Mail order\telephone order – MOTO) transactions.

- The SAQ B-IP doesn't apply to eCommerce channel merchants.

- A merchant is required to respond to 80+ questions, with explanations for any questions that do not apply to their environment.

- The merchant uses only approved payment terminals (PTS POI devices) that are standalone and connected to the payment processor via the internet.

- These devices are validated and listed on the PCI SSC website. They are not connected to any other systems in the merchant's environment, which can be achieved through network segmentation.

- The payment information is transmitted only from the approved devices to the payment processor. The PTS POI devices do not depend on any other devices like computers, mobile phones, or tablets to connect to the payment processor.

IP-connected devices are essential for businesses that want to securely and efficiently process payments. By isolating them from the rest of the network, companies are adding an extra layer of security to their CDE.

Internet Protocol (IP) connected devices are allocated a fixed IP address by the Network or IT Security team. They will designate a range of IP addresses for use in these devices. This range of IPs will be segmented and protected from the wider network, thus reducing the PCI-DSS scope.

Connected IP devices, such as electronic card swipe machines, integrated payment applications, or tills, are essential components of a secure and compliant payment processing infrastructure. By isolating these devices from the rest of the network, they become a fortress - a secure environment where payments can be processed securely.

Tip: If using a Chip & PIN device over a mobile network (payment device with a SIM card), then SAQ B would be applicable. The data traverses the mobile web and isn't managed by the merchant.

SAQ (C-VT)

- SAQ (C-VT) applies to those merchants using an Internet-based virtual terminal solution provided and hosted by a third-party service provider that has been PCI-DSS validated.

- Merchants manually enter a single transaction at a time using a keyboard into an Internet-based virtual terminal solution. It should be noted that these merchants can handle both card-present and card-not-present transactions and do not store any card information on their computers.

- SAQ C-VT doesn't apply to eCommerce environments.

- These merchants can handle both card-present (brick-and-mortar) and card-not-present (Mail order\telephone order – MOTO) transactions.

- A merchant is required to respond to just over 80 questions, with explanations for any questions that are not applicable to their environment.

- You will typically find these types of merchants in customer service departments, dedicated call centers, and mail-order organizations. The operator would normally take the card details from the customer over the telephone, then enter them into the virtual payment terminal solution.

- The benefit of this is that the PCI-DSS network scope is reduced significantly, allowing for a much safer environment. With the proper configuration and protection, you can rest assured knowing your virtual payment system is safe and secure.

- Make sure these types of payment calls are not recorded. Recording them would extend your PCI-DSS network scope. There are technical solutions available whereby an operator can pause the call recording while the payment is taken. This way, you can ensure that the personal information of your customers is not exposed and that your PCI-DSS network remains within its designated scope. This is one of the most efficient and secure methods for protecting customer payment information. It's an easy way to show that you value their privacy and security while protecting your assets.

- The only way to process payments is through a virtual payment terminal that can be accessed using an Internet-connected web browser. A third-party service provider hosts the virtual payment terminal solution, which is PCI DSS compliant. To ensure security, the virtual payment terminal solution can only be accessed using a computing device that is isolated in a single location and not connected to other systems. The computing device does not have any software or hardware devices that capture or store account data.

SAQ (C)

- SAQ (C) merchants process cardholder data (CHD) via point-of-sale (POS) or other payment application systems connected to the internet.

- The SAQ-C is applicable when using an installed payment processing application on a computer, laptop, tablet, in stores, or on a till.

- These merchants can handle both card-present (brick-and-mortar) and card-not-present (Mail order\telephone order – MOTO) transactions.

- It can't be used for eCommerce transactions.

The process is straightforward. Merchants enter the CHD into the POS system, or it could be entered by the customer using Chip & PIN or contactless. The payment application then securely encrypts the cardholder data (CHD) and forwards it to the appropriate payment processor. This ensures that the customer's data is kept safe and secure.

A merchant is required to respond to 160+ questions, with explanations for any questions that do not apply to their environment.

The merchant's device has both a payment application system and an Internet connection. However, the payment application system is not linked to any other systems in the merchant's environment. This can be achieved through network segmentation. Also, the POS environment is physically isolated from other premises or locations. Finally, any LAN is used only for a single store. Retail systems can quickly meet this criteria. However, integrated systems may need help meeting it.

SAQ-(P2PE)

- These merchants can handle both card-present (brick-and-mortar) and card-not-present (Mail order\telephone order – MOTO) transactions. For example when taking an order over the phone and keying in the card information directly into a PCI listed P2PE payment terminal.

- This SAQ does not cover E-commerce channels.

- The merchant must be using a PCI-validated P2PE solution and have successfully implemented it.

- Merchants must respond to 30+ questions, explaining any questions that do not apply to their business environment.

P2PE utilizes a secure form of asymmetrical encryption to protect cardholder data, ensuring it remains secure throughout its journey. Like an unbreakable vault, it is locked at the Chip & PIN device point of collection and only unlocked at its final destination. This ensures the data remains safe from prying eyes and malicious intent, providing a secure payment processing experience.

- Please keep in mind that it is expensive to implement this P2PE solution, and it is aimed at medium to large retail chains.

- The solution is fully managed and patched by a third-party solution provider. This means that you do not need to worry about any of the technical aspects of the solution.

- This is an excellent choice for merchants who want to keep their data safe and secure without worrying about technicalities.

- The implementation of a P2PE solution can reduce the time required to perform a full PCI-DSS audit to just a few days.

SAQ-(D) Merchants

SAQ-(D) An SAQ D is your only option if none of the SAQs already mentioned meet your organization's criteria.

To comply with SAQ D, merchants must comply with all 12 PCI-DSS requirements and its 300+ sub-requirements.

All questions must be answered by merchants, with explanations for any questions that do not apply to their business practices.

- As another consideration, if you have multiple payment channels that require multiple SAQs with a lot of overlap, it may be simpler for you to complete SAQ D for all your payment channels.

The security of payment channels can be a tricky business. It's like a high-stakes game of chess, where every move matters, and a single misstep can have disastrous consequences. But with the right strategy, you can keep your payment channels safe and secure.

SAQ D may be used in several merchant environments, including, but not limited to:

- Merchants who accept cardholder data on their websites.

- Cardholder data is stored electronically by merchants.

- Those merchants who do not store cardholder data electronically but do not meet the criteria of another SAQ type.

- Merchants who may meet the criteria of another SAQ type but have additional PCI-DSS requirements.

SAQ D may be used by merchants who accept cardholder data on their websites, store cardholder data electronically, or have additional PCI-DSS requirements.

TIP: An SAQ D should be avoided if at all possible by any merchant. By examining the payment channels in use, you can deter-

mine how your organization handles payment card information, make changes to secure your cardholder data environment (CDE), and potentially reduce the PCI-DSS scope.

SAQ-(D) Service Providers

SAQ-(D) An SAQ D is the only option for Service Providers and is a lengthy document.

A service provider must answer all questions and explain any questions that do not pertain to their business practices.

However, it's worth pointing out that service providers are entitled to decide which of their services are to be compliant. This is especially applicable for hosting providers that provide many different services, and it may well be the case that not all services are required to be compliant.

Tip: If you store cardholder data (CHD) digitally, you must complete SAQ D.

Payment Card Industry Data Security Standard Version: 4.0

Self-Assessment Questionnaires at a Glance

SAQ-A

Card-not-present merchants (e-commerce or mail/telephone-order), that have fully outsourced all cardholder data function to PCI-DSS compliant third-party service providers, with no electronic storage, processing, or transmission of any cardholder data on the merchant's systems or premises.

SAQ-A-ES

E-Commerce merchants who outsource all payment processing to PCI-DSS validated third-parties, and who have a website(s) that doesn't directly receive cardholder data but that can impact the security of the payment transaction. No electronic storage, processing, or transmission of any cardholder data on the merchant's systems or premises.

Applicable only to e-commerce channels

SAQ-B

Merchants using only:
Imprint machines with no electronic cardholder data storage, and/or
Standalone, dial-out terminals with no electronic cardholder data storage.

SAQ-B-IP

Merchants using only standalone, PTS-approved payment terminals with an IP connection to the payment processor with no electronic cardholder data storage.

Not applicable to e-commerce channels

SAQ-C-VT

Merchants who manually enter a single transaction at a time via a keyboard into an Internet-based, virtual payment terminal solution that is provided and hosted by a PCI-DSS validated third-party service provider. No electronic cardholder data storage.

SAQ-C

Merchants with payment application systems connected to the internet, with no electronic cardholder data storage.

Not applicable to e-commerce channels

SAQ-P2PE

Merchants using only hardware payment terminals included in and managed via a validated, PCI SSC-listed Point-to-Point Encryption (P2PE) solution, with no electronic cardholder data storage.

Not applicable to e-commerce channels

SAQ-D - For Merchants
All merchants not included in descriptions for the above SAQ types

SAQ-D - For Service Providers
All service providers defined by a payment brand as eligible to complete an SAQ

Self-Assessment Questionnaires

Summary

The PCI-DSS Self-Assessment Questionnaires (SAQs) are for merchants and service providers to guide them on their compliance journey. All of the SAQs are designed for different types of merchants and service providers and their cardholder data environments. These questionnaires require responses to various questions associated with specific requirements to ensure cardholder data security. The SAQs help you to state to your acquirer how you are complying with the PCI DSS. SAQ D is the only option if none of the other SAQs meet an organization's criteria.

CHAPTER 24

AoC & RoC Compliance

Attestation of Compliance (AoC)

The Attestation of Compliance (AoC) is a certification that specifies an organization's PCI-DSS compliance status and is completed and verified by a Qualified Security Assessor (QSA). A PCI AoC proves an organization supports security best practices. An AoC is a powerful written statement that assures your organization has completed a valid SAQ or PCI assessment tailored to your cardholder environment.

Report on Compliance (RoC)

A Report on Compliance (RoC) outlines an organization's security posture, environment, systems, and cardholder data protection; it confirms whether the PCI requirements are being met.

RoCs are required for all Level 1 merchants. A PCI Level 1 merchant is a retailer that processes more than 6 million Visa or Mastercard transactions annually.

In Practice

Following the testing of your controls and the collection of documentation of your processes, a PCI auditor (QSA) creates a final PCI RoC (Report on Compliance).

A Report on Compliance is a document that documents the detailed results of an assessment of PCI-DSS compliance; it is then presented to the merchant's acquirer.

As soon as the acquirer has accepted the RoC, it then sends it to the payment brand for verification.

Summary

The Payment Card Industry Data Security Standard (PCI-DSS) requires organizations to demonstrate compliance with its security requirements through an Attestation of Compliance (AoC) or a Report on Compliance (RoC). An AoC certifies a company's compliance with PCI-DSS and is completed by a Qualified Security Assessor (QSA). An RoC outlines an organization's security posture, environment, systems, and cardholder data protection. RoCs are required for all Level 1 merchants who process more than 6 million Visa or Mastercard transactions annually. After an audit, the QSA prepares an RoC, which must be presented to the merchant's acquirer and sent to the payment brand for verification.

CHAPTER 25

PRIORITIZED APPROACH TOOL (PAT)

Organizations can prioritize compliance efforts by identifying quick wins by utilizing the Prioritised Approach Tool. This encourages you and helps you track the progress of your PCI-DSS compliance program.

The tool aims to assist you with your compliance journey, through a set of security milestones designed to lower the risk of a data breach.

Using this tool, the business can keep track of its compliance against each PCI-DSS control and document its progress against those controls. The tool also helps you identify gaps in your compliance program and areas where you may need to focus your efforts.

The Prioritised Approach Tool (PAT) is a valuable tool for you as a PCIP, as you may not necessarily be a project manager, so this tool is ideal for you as you chart your compliance progress.

Unleashing the Power of Prioritization: The PAT Tool's Six Areas in Order of Importance

1. Data retention should be limited, and sensitive authentication data (SAD) should be removed from the system as soon as possible.

2. Ensure that your systems and networks are protected in case of a data breach.

3. Applications that securely accept payment cards.

4. It is important to monitor and control who has access to your systems.

5. It is important to protect the data pertaining to cardholders.

6. The remaining compliance efforts need to be completed, and all controls need to be in place.

Summary

The Prioritized Approach Tool (PAT) helps organizations prioritize their compliance efforts by identifying quick wins and tracking progress against PCI-DSS controls. It aims to protect cardholder data and sensitive authentication data through security milestones. The tool helps identify gaps in compliance programs and areas that require focus. The PAT is ideal for PCIPs to prioritize activities and meet deadlines. Six areas are prioritized, including limiting data retention, protecting systems in case of a breach, securely accepting payment cards, monitoring system access, protecting cardholder data, and completing the remaining compliance efforts.

CHAPTER 26

USER AUTHENTICATION AND PASSWORD SECURITY

The security of customer data is paramount for any organization that processes payments using debit or credit cards. To comply with PCI-DSS and to ensure the highest level of protection, organizations must implement stringent security policies to create a safe and secure cardholder data environment. Think of it like a fortress— With the right approach, you can ensure that your customers' information is secured and protected from malicious activity.

Tip: Understand and memorize the following information.

User Authentication

Combining user IDs with these additional authentication methods provides a robust level of security for anyone accessing cardholder data (non-consumer users and administrators).

Something you know: This is the most common form of authentication and requires users to provide a username and a passphrase or a password.

Something you have: This requires users to have a token device or smart card.

Tip: If you're looking for a secure way to prove your identity online, a digital certificate might be just what you need! This nifty little tool serves as a form of "something you have" - an added layer of security that confirms you are who you say you are. It's important to note that for a digital certificate to be effective, it needs to be personalized to you and only you - no sharing allowed! So if you're ready to up your online security game, consider getting yourself a unique digital certificate.

Something you are: This form of authentication requires users to provide a biometric identifier, such as a fingerprint or a facial scan.

Unique User ID's

Assign all users a unique ID before allowing them to access systems connected to the cardholder data environment. This ID must be unique within your organization and different from the user's name or other identifiers. Once these users leave the business, all access to their unique IDs must be revoked immediately.

Remove, or Disable inactive user accounts within 90 days.

Tip: Only allow 'Just in Time' (JIT) access for third party user IDs and monitor their usage.

Password Policy

First of all, unique passwords are a requirement in any organization, regardless of whether there is a cardholder data environment. This means all shared, generic and default passwords are not permitted! These should all be removed or disabled from any new systems or applications, or if found on existing systems and applications, removed immediately (following any Change Management processes that may be in place).

Password complexity, history, lockout periods, and password age all come into play when having a secure environment. Password security is the key to keeping your data safe and secure. It's like having a fortress around your information, protecting it from any malicious attempts to access it. With password complexity, history, lockout periods, and password age all playing a role, you can be sure your data is safe from unwanted intruders.

Think of these security measures as a set of locks on your door. The more complex the password, the harder it is for someone to guess it and gain access. The same goes for password history and lockout periods - if someone tries to guess your password multiple times, they will be locked out for a certain period.

Finally, password age helps to ensure that passwords are regularly updated and kept fresh. This prevents hackers from using old passwords that may have been compromised in a past data breach.

Complex Passwords & Passphrases

Passwords and passphrases are usually made up of letters, numbers, and special characters, while passphrases are generally much longer and may contain both the attributes of a password and spaces.

PCI-DSS requires **passwords and passphrases to be at least twelve characters long**, and they must include both **alphabetic and numeric** characters. Alternatively, passwords and passphrases should have at least the same level of complexity and strength as the parameters above to ensure they are secure.

Note that a minimum of eight characters is allowed if legacy systems don't support using such long passwords or passphrases.

Lockout periods

After **ten failed attempts**, lock out the user ID to limit repeated access attempts. Lock out the user ID for at least **30 minutes** or until an administrator enables it.

Idle Sessions

To re-activate a terminal or session that has been inactive for more than **15 minutes**, ask the user to re-authenticate so that the terminal or session can be activated again. In some organizations, the allowed idle time could be less than the 15-minute requirement and include activation of the screensaver.

Password age

You should change your passwords or passphrases **at least once every 90 days.** See requirements 8.3.9 through 8.3.10.1 for additional information.

Password History

PCI-DSS requires that you do not allow an individual to submit a new password or passphrase that is the same as any of the **last 4 passwords or passphrases** they have previously used. This protects against **brute force attacks** and other forms of **credential stuffing.**

Password Hygiene

You should require passwords and passphrases to be reset for **first-time use**, as well as when they are reset, make sure a unique value is used for each user. The user should **change them immediately after the first use.** It is strongly advised that you do not use any commonly known passwords such as LetMeIn123 or Password1234.

All Non-console (Remote Access) to the CDE for personnel with administrative access rights must be protected by **multi-factor authentication.**

All **ACCESS** to the CDE must be protected by **multi-factor authentication.**

The security of your CDE is paramount, and multi-factor authentication is a powerful tool to keep it safe. It's like having an extra layer of armor protecting your system from malicious intent. This protection extends to onsite and remote access, ensuring that everyone with access is held to the highest security standards.

By using these security measures together, you can ensure your data is safe and secure from any unwanted intruders. It's like having an impenetrable fortress around your information - no one can get in without the right combination of locks!

Summary

To ensure the highest level of protection for your cardholder data, you must implement stringent security policies. Your password should be complex and changed at least once every 90 days. After ten failed attempts, lock out the user ID for at least 30 minutes or until an administrator enables it. Re-authenticate after an idle session of more than 15 minutes. Do not use commonly known passwords such as LetMeIn123 or Password1234. All non-console accesses to the CDE should be protected by multi-factor authentication, ensuring everyone with administrative access is held to the highest security standards.

CHAPTER 27

THE EXCITING JOURNEY OF PCI DSS CHANGES: A LIFECYCLE OVERVIEW

The PCI-DSS Lifecycle, with its eight stages, has a duration of 36 months and follows a predefined path, with each stage having specific steps and deliverables. The PCI-DSS Lifecycle Model helps the PCI SSC assess its current PCI-DSS standards. This assessment is done through reviews, updates, and revisions. Over the various stages of the Lifecycle, the PCI SSC is busily working towards bringing the PCI-DSS standards up to date. Ensuring that the new standards address the evolving technologies and threats as they appear. Through reviews, updates, and revisions, this model ensures that your business stays ahead of the game and remains at the forefront of security.

The PCI-DSS Lifecycle Model helps the PCI SSC assess its current PCI-DSS standards.

If you aren't aware of the changes in the PCI standards, let me take you on a journey through the 36-month Lifecycle with its eight stages.

The Eight Stages

1. **Standards Published:** Stage 1 of the PCI DSS lifecycle occurs in October, right after the Council's annual Community Meetings. This stage marks the beginning of a fresh cycle for PCI DSS. As a stakeholder, you have the freedom to implement the new standards immediately, but it is not mandatory until they

become effective. This gives you ample time to understand and prepare for the recent changes. It also allows you to take a measured approach to ensure that your organization is fully equipped to adopt the new standards with minimal disruption to your business operations. By taking advantage of this time, you can ensure that you are fully compliant with the PCI DSS regulations, which will help you safeguard your business against potential security breaches and protect your customers' sensitive data.

2. **Standards Effective:** With Stage 2, the new PCI DSS standards become effective on January 1 of Year 1, and stakeholders should start using them for their payment security programs. The old standards are grandfathered for 14 months for compliance validation, but it's recommended to transition to the new standards quickly, especially for critical control requirements.

3. **Market Implementation:** In Stage 3, the market fully embraces the new standards. This means evaluating how the changes affect a stakeholder's cardholder data environment. Stage 3 spans Year 1 and ensures a smooth and gradual integration of necessary updates. So, get ready to experience a seamless transition to the latest industry standards!

4. **Feedback Begins:** During Stage 4 of this Lifecycle, which takes place from November to March of Year 2, stakeholders are invited to provide feedback on any new standards and suggest improvements. This is a valuable opportunity for stakeholders to share their insights and contribute to the ongoing development of the PCI DSS. The Council will then carefully consider all feedback submitted and communicate how it will be incorporated into future versions of the standards.

5. **Old Standards Retired:** Stage 5 marks an important milestone in the world of payment security and is slated to take place on the last day of December in Year 2. It is imperative to note that this date is of paramount significance, as it marks the official retirement of the outdated PCI DSS standards. This event represents a crucial step towards enhancing the overall security posture of payment systems. Organizations must stay abreast of this development to comply with the latest industry standards. Therefore, it is essential to be mindful of this date and take appropriate measures to ensure that your payment systems are updated and

secured in accordance with the new standards.

6. **Feedback Review:** Stage 6 of the PCI DSS lifecycle happens from April through August of Year 2. It involves collecting and evaluating feedback from Participating Organizations. Feedback is categorized into three types: clarifications, additional guidance, and evolving requirements. The goal is to ensure concise wording portrays the desired intent of requirements, provide further information on a particular topic, and ensure standards are up to date with emerging threats and changes in the market.

7. **Draft Revisions:** Welcome to Stage 7, where things move up a notch! The PCI SSC share that they are drafting new standards grounded in thorough research, analysis, and input from their valued stakeholders. The Technical Working Group is hard at work during this stage, preparing drafts that will be circulated internally for review by the Council. This all happens between November and April in Year 3.

8. **Final Review:** The process for changes to PCI-DSS involve the seven stages mentioned above, with the final stage, Stage 8, concerning the review and adjustment of drafts by the Council and Board of Advisors. A "summary of changes" document is provided to stakeholders, and the final versions are prepared for publication at Community Meetings. This occurs from May through July of Year 3, and a new three-year lifecycle begins upon publication on the Council's website.

The PCI Lifecycle Model is available to view in the PCI SSC document library: https://www.pcisecuritystandards.org/document_library/

Type lifecycle in the search window and tick Show Archived Documents.

Summary

The PCI-DSS has a 36-month lifecycle with eight stages, starting in October after the Council's annual Community Meetings. Organizations should transition to new standards quickly, especially for critical control requirements. Stakeholders can provide feedback during Stage 4 from November to March of Year 2. Stage 5 marks the official retirement of outdated PCI DSS standards on the last day of December in Year 2. Stage 6 happens from April through August of Year 2, and the final stage involves the review and adjustment of drafts by the Council and Board of Advisors from May through July of Year 3.

CHAPTER 28

ADDITIONAL TECHNOLOGY INFORMATION

Business As Usual (BAU)

To effectively integrate PCI-DSS into business-as-usual processes, the following best practices should be followed:

PCI-DSS is much more than just monitoring once a year and getting ready for a point-in-time test day at the end of the year.

Compliance does not necessarily indicate security, so focus on your organization's compliance and security aspects.

By integrating security into standard business processes, organizations can maintain a PCI-DSS-compliant environment between PCI-DSS assessments.

Remember that the people in your organization also play an essential role in maintaining your PCI-DSS-compliant status, so make sure everyone in your organization is aware of their role.

The Benefits of Implementing Network Segregation

The first thing to mention about network segregation is that implementing it will limit or reduce the scope of PCI-DSS assessments. This means that you will be able to focus on the most critical aspects of your business, such as ensuring that your CDE is secure.

As well as the obvious cost savings associated with a reduced assessment, implementing network segregation can reduce the complexity associated with implementing and maintaining PCI-DSS security controls. By dividing your network into separate zones, you can better control access to sensitive data and mitigate risks to your organization. Not only does network segregation reduce scope, but it also makes it easier to identify and troubleshoot security incidents. In the event of a breach, only one section of the network might be affected, making it easier to contain and resolve the issue quickly.

Let's take a real-world example. Imagine you run a small online retail store. You accept credit card payments through your website but use a tablet in-store to process payments. By implementing network segregation, you can ensure that only the devices and payment channels in scope are adequately secured and compliant with PCI-DSS. This protects your customers' sensitive information and saves you time and money by reducing the scope of your assessments.

Tokenization

Tokenization replaces sensitive data, such as a PAN, with a unique, non-sensitive surrogate value called a token.

If you choose to store tokens instead of PANs, you can reduce the amount of cardholder data in your environment and simultaneously reduce the scope of your PCI-DSS compliance. It is important to note, however, that tokenization does not remove the need to comply with PCI-DSS.

Beware of a token called a 'high-value token.' This token category can be used to retrieve PAN or perform transactions. Accordingly, a high-value token could have the same sensitivity as PAN and, therefore, fall under the scope of PCI-DSS.

Many tokenization solutions are on the market, but not all are created equal. Organizations should make sure that they evaluate and apply risk analysis to ensure the tokenization solution meets their requirements in terms of functionality and security.

Tokenization can provide an extra layer of security, allowing organizations to reduce the amount of cardholder data in their environment and reduce the scope of their PCI-DSS compliance. With the right tokenization solution, organizations can feel confident that their data is safe and secure.

Virtualization

The concept of virtualization is the separation of applications, desktops, machines, networks, data, and services from their corresponding physical constraints. Virtualization is a way to increase the efficiency of an organization's computing resources by allowing multiple applications and services to run on a single physical server. Virtualization also provides an extra layer of security, isolating applications and data from each other so that if one application or service is compromised, the rest remain secure.

Think of virtualization as a bridge between the physical and digital worlds. It combines the power of physical servers with the flexibility of the cloud, creating a powerful combination that can help organizations get more out of their computing resources.

Virtualization is an incredibly powerful concept that can help organizations save time, money, and resources. With virtualization, organizations can do more with less, freeing up their computing resources for other tasks. By unlocking the potential of their computing resources, organizations can focus on what matters most: growing their business.

Remember that PCI-DSS still applies when applying virtualization technologies to your cardholder data environment.

Additionally, there are several pertinent considerations to be aware of:

- As with any evolving technology, there are associated risks. By understanding the risks associated with virtualization, a PCIP can help an organization make the most informed decisions about its adoption.

- When virtualizing a cardholder data environment, it is crucial to consider the impact of virtualization on PCI-DSS compliance.

Point to Point Encryption (P2PE)

Encryption is a powerful tool for protecting data and ensuring privacy. It is like a digital lock that only the intended recipient can unlock. It works by scrambling data so that it can only be accessed with the correct key. Encryption is essential to cybersecurity, allowing us to protect our sensitive information from prying eyes and malicious actors. It is a powerful tool for keeping private information out of the wrong hands.

In the context of a P2PE solution, card transactions are encrypted at one designated and independently validated encryption device. To decrypt the data, the encrypted ciphertext is sent to a second designated and independently validated device capable of decrypting the unreadable ciphertext. While the data is in transit between the source and the destination, it remains encrypted, with no possibility of decryption at any point along the way.

Encryption is a powerful ally in the fight against cybercrime and digital espionage, and P2PE is an essential part of that fight.

Mobile Devices

It won't have escaped your notice that credit or debit card payments can be made in the middle of a field (providing there's a signal) at a farmers market, pop-up shop, or even at the table of your favorite restaurant. All this is made possible with the introduction of mobile technologies.

Mobile devices have revolutionized the way we live and work. They allow us to stay connected wherever we are and conduct business transactions without leaving our comfort zones.

The popularity of mobile devices has led to the development of a range of applications that can be used to make our lives easier.

Several devices have been specifically designed to conduct business transactions. These include handheld devices such as mobile phones, tablets and iPads with payment software installed, connected to an addon device. Handheld PoS devices will accept contactless payments using Near Field Communication (NFC), or allow you to swipe your credit or debit card.

Merchants use these mobile technologies to streamline their payment processes wherever possible. Despite this increase in convenience at the point of sale, mobile payment acceptance can also present a new set of risks regarding the security of cardholder data.

The mobile device is a powerful and versatile tool that can be used in many ways. However, it is essential to remember that they are not designed to provide secure input or storage of cardholder information. To ensure that cardholder data remains safe, it is essential to use other methods, such as encryption and tokenization, to protect sensitive information. By taking these extra steps, we can ensure that our customer's data is kept secure and protected.

There are several ways to offer secure mobile payment options. It all starts with a point of interaction (POI). An approved PIN entry device (PED) or a secure card reader (SCR) captures and encrypts the cardholder's information.

A POI device that has been approved is designed exclusively to capture and encrypt cardholder data safely and securely. A list of approved devices and P2PE solutions will be available on the PCI SSC website as soon as they become validated.

Wi-Fi

Let's talk about Wi-Fi and how it impacts PCI-DSS in the context of credit cards.

First things first, Wi-Fi can be a real game-changer when it comes to credit card transactions. It allows for quick and easy payments, which is great for both customers and businesses. However, it also poses some security risks that need to be addressed in order to comply with PCI-DSS standards.

One of the biggest concerns with Wi-Fi is the potential for unauthorized access to sensitive information. If someone gains access to your Wi-Fi network, they could potentially intercept credit card data as it's being transmitted. This is obviously a huge problem, as it puts both your customers and your business at risk.

To address this issue, PCI-DSS requires that any Wi-Fi networks used for credit card transactions be secured using strong encryption methods. This means using WPA2 or higher encryption protocols and implementing strong passwords and other security measures.

Let's take a look at a real-world example of how this might work. Imagine you run a small coffee shop that accepts credit card payments via Wi-Fi. To comply with PCI-DSS standards, you must ensure that your Wi-Fi network is secured using WPA2 encryption and a strong password. You must also regularly monitor your network for any signs of unauthorized access or suspicious activity.

By taking these steps, you can help ensure that your customers' credit card data remains safe and secure while still enjoying the convenience of Wi-Fi payments.

Bluetooth

Bluetooth technology has certainly made our lives easier, but it's important to keep in mind that convenience can come with risks.

To ensure the safety of wireless communication and comply with PCI-DSS standards, businesses must take proactive measures. Fortunately, several types of Bluetooth PoS devices are available in the market that can help businesses protect their customers' data.

These devices range from handheld terminals to countertop models, each with unique features and benefits. Handheld terminals are ideal for mobile businesses or those with limited counter space, while countertop models are better suited for larger establishments.

Additionally, some Bluetooth PoS devices offer advanced security features such as encryption and tokenization to safeguard sensitive information further. By choosing the right type of Bluetooth PoS device for their business needs, companies can ensure the security of their customers' data while still enjoying the convenience of wireless technology.

Near Field Communication (NFC)

Near Field Communication (NFC) is a technology that allows two devices to communicate wirelessly when they are in close proximity. This technology has become increasingly popular in recent years, especially in the context of credit cards.

NFC-enabled credit cards use radio frequency identification (RFID) technology to transmit payment information wirelessly between the card and the payment terminal. This means that customers can tap their card on the terminal to make a payment without swiping or inserting their card.

However, this convenience also comes with some security risks. Hackers can use specialized equipment to intercept and steal the payment information transmitted by NFC-enabled cards. To mitigate this risk, PCI-DSS requires merchants to implement additional security measures when processing NFC transactions.

A real-world example of NFC in action is contactless payments at a coffee shop. Imagine you're in a rush and need your caffeine fix before work. You grab your NFC-enabled credit card and tap it on the payment terminal at the counter. Within seconds, your payment is processed, and you're on your way with your coffee in hand. All thanks to the magic of NFC!

Biometric Authentication

Biometric authentication is a security method that uses unique physical characteristics to verify a person's identity. This can include fingerprints, facial recognition, voice recognition, and even the way a person types on a keyboard. Biometric authentication is becoming increasingly popular because it is much harder to hack or replicate than traditional passwords or PINs. Biometric authentication is one of the strongest authentication methods available. Biometric authentication is a powerful tool in the fight against credit card fraud. By using unique physical characteristics to verify a person's identity, companies can better protect the cardholder data environment and meet PCI-DSS security standards for entry points in a cardholder data environment or card production facilities.

Summary

This chapter discussed the importance of integrating PCI-DSS into business-as-usual processes and provides best practices for doing so. It emphasizes that PCI-DSS is more than just a yearly monitoring and testing process. It also highlights the importance of encrypting data in transit and mentions the potential risks associated with mobile payment acceptance.

CHAPTER SUMMARIES

Overview of the PCIP Qualification

The Payment Card Industry Security Standards Council offers the PCIP certification program to deepen your knowledge of the payments ecosystem and develop your payment card security knowledge. Once certified, individuals can apply PCI standards to support their organization's or clients' ongoing security and compliance efforts. The program also makes individuals experts in the essential set of security standards known as PCI-DSS, enabling them to protect cardholder data and reduce the risk of fraud. The certification process involves outlining work experience and passing an exam through Pearson VUE, either online or in person. The learning objectives include developing a fundamental understanding of the payment card industry, PCI standards, and how PCI DSS applies to cardholder data.

ISA, QSA & PCIP: Unlocking the Path to Success

This chapter discussed three certifications that can help professionals advance their careers in the payment card industry: PCI-QSA, PCI-ISA, and PCIP. PCI-ISA is for information security team members who want to enhance their knowledge of PCI Security Standards and ensure their company meets requirements. PCI-QSA is for those associated with a company conducting PCI-DSS assessments. PCIP is for professionals in the payment card industry to showcase their expertise in PCI-DSS Standards and supporting materials. All three certifications require passing an examination and may require additional training courses. Obtaining these certifications can help professionals stand out in the job market and enhance their knowledge of data security standards.

The Evolution of the Payment Card Industry

When protecting our credit card information, we all want peace of mind. Fortunately, there's a framework in place that's always on top of the latest industry trends and practices - the Payment Card Industry Data Security Standard (PCI-DSS 4.0). By following these requirements, businesses can show their commitment to safeguarding sensitive data and give customers the reassurance they need. It's a must for any organization handling credit card payments, and non-compliance can lead to penalties or even losing the ability to process payments. Luckily, the PCI Security Standards Council offers training and certification services to help businesses stay compliant. So next time you swipe your card, rest easy knowing your data is in good hands.

The Payment Brands

Five of the biggest payment brands in the world established the Payment Card Industry Security Standards Council: American Express, Discover Financial Services, JCB International, MasterCard Worldwide, and Visa International (UnionPay is a recent addition). Each brand has a unique data security compliance program and responsibilities adhering to the PCI-DSS. These include monitoring and enforcing security measures, imposing penalties and fees for non-compliance, carrying out validation processes, and defining the levels of merchants and service providers. The payment brands are not just figureheads - they play a critical role in ensuring that all validation documentation is of high quality and in responding to data breaches. Think of them as guardians who closely monitor account data to ensure that all security standards are met.

The Hidden Dangers of Ignoring the PCI-Data Security Standard

This chapter discussed the importance of implementing PCI-DSS guidelines to protect against potential threats to cardholder data. Cybercriminals often target payment card data and use various methods, such as skimming, phishing, malware, and contactless payment fraud, to steal sensitive information. Insider threats are also significant, where employees mishandle or steal credit card information. It is crucial to secure not only your systems but also those of any third-party vendors or contractors with access to sensitive data. Implementing robust authentication protocols, closely monitoring vendor access, and conducting thorough background checks on contractors and vendors can help safeguard valuable cardholder data. Failure to comply with these requirements can result in hefty fines and damage your reputation as a business owner.

Unveiling the Intricacies of the Payment Card Ecosystem

The world of payment cards is a bustling network of institutions and companies working together to secure transactions. This ecosystem involves banks, credit card companies, and merchants collaborating to create a platform for seamless card payments. This system allows shoppers to use their cards to make purchases, while merchants can easily accept them. The payment card network also plays a crucial role in processing payments, which is an essential part of the global economy. The key players in this ecosystem include cardholders, issuers\banks, acquirers\banks, and the six payment brands: Visa, Mastercard, Discover, JCB, American Express and more recently, UnionPay. Understanding this ecosystem is vital for managing PCI compliance risks and acing the PCIP exam.

The Puzzle of Connections: Understanding How It All Fits Together

This content explains the different players involved in the payment card ecosystem, including the acquiring bank, payment brands, interchange rates, assessment fees, issuing banks, and merchants. The acquiring bank holds a merchant's funds and offers them card readers to process credit card transactions. Payment brands set interchange rates and assessment fees that impact transaction costs. Interchange rates are fees charged for processing transactions between issuing banks and merchants, while assessment fees are additional charges for payment brand services. The issuing bank verifies the cardholder's identity and confirms sufficient funds to complete a transaction. Merchants accept cards from various payment brands and drive growth in the industry.

Unlocking the Secrets of the Card Payment Process

Paying with your credit card involves several steps to ensure a smooth and secure transaction. When you present and swipe your card, a chain of authorization takes place, ultimately obtaining approval from your issuing bank. This bank then verifies your card number, CVV, customer address, and available funds to authenticate the transaction. Finally, the merchant performs batch processing, which includes Clearing and Settlement. It's important to note that this payment card ecosystem is complex. Still, by following the established process, you can trust that your credit card information is being handled safely and securely.

Understanding Card Security Codes and Their Usage Across Different Brands

Different payment card brands have different security codes to verify transactions. American Express and Discover cards have a 4-digit CID on the front of the card, JCB cards have a 3-digit CAV2 on the back, MasterCard has a 3-digit CVC2 on the back, and Visa has a 3-digit CVV2 on the back. UnionPay has a 3-digit CVN on the back of the card. Knowing these codes and their locations is essential for the PCIP examination.

PCI-DSS Applicability Information

To ensure secure payment card processing, merchants and service providers must comply with the Payment Card Industry Data Security Standard. This includes safeguarding cardholder data and sensitive authentication data (SAD). Outsourcing payment operations or the cardholder data environment (CDE) management to third parties does not exempt an organization from PCI-DSS requirements. Storing SAD after authorization is not allowed, but if stored can put customers' data at risk of being compromised by hackers. Protecting customers' data is crucial for avoiding chargebacks, loss of revenue, and damage to a business's reputation.

PCI-DSS Standards

As a reminder, PCI-DSS applies to all entities involved in payment card processing, including merchants, processors, acquirers, issuers, and service providers. It covers security for any system components connected to the cardholder data environment (CDE). As part of PCI-DSS, the P2PE, PTS, SSF, and PCI PIN requirements are incorporated to ensure account data is protected from the moment it is captured until it reaches the payment processor. In the Payment Card Industry, Data Security standards are an essential set of security standards designed to process and store payment card information securely. This comprehensive set of standards helps protect cardholder data from theft, fraud, and misuse. It also ensures that businesses meet the highest data security standards. Businesses must be diligent in adhering to the PCI-DSS standards to remain compliant and protect their customers' data. Compliance with the PCI-DSS standards can help companies build trust with their customers and ensure their data remains safe and secure.

It's a critical component of any business's security strategy and is essential for protecting cardholder data from malicious actors.

PCI Code of Professional Responsibility

The PCI Code of Professional Responsibility is a set of principles that all professionals in the payment card industry must follow to ensure that payment card data is handled securely, ethically, and responsibly. It outlines expectations for professionals to maintain high standards of conduct and comply with all PCI Standards and guidelines. The Code serves as a beacon of trust for all parties involved in the payment card industry, ensuring their data is secure. Violations of the Code may result in disciplinary action such as warnings, suspension, or revocation of PCI SSC qualification. As a PCIP, one must strive to uphold the highest standards of conduct and provide diligent and competent customer service while following all PCI Standards, guidelines, and procedures.

Scoping Your Connected Environment

Scoping is critical in understanding the cardholder data environment (CDE) and ensuring compliance with security requirements. Before a PCI-DSS assessment, entities must verify the accuracy of their scope by identifying all locations and flows of cardholder data. Introducing controls such as outsourcing online ordering can reduce the scope and simplify compliance efforts. To confirm the accuracy of the defined CDE, the assessed entity must identify and document all cardholder data in its environment and verify that no cardholder data exists outside of it.

Consequences of Non-Compliance to PCI-DSS

Non-compliance with PCI-DSS can result in penalties, fines, and even being banned from accepting credit card transactions. A breach of personal information must be reported within 72 hours, and credit card brands can transfer the cost of credit card replacement to you if you're in breach. You could also be held liable for any fraudulent transactions resulting from a leak. It's crucial to implement the highest level of security protocols and procedures to protect customer data. Compliance once a year with PCI-DSS is not enough; regular testing for vulnerabilities should be regarded as a business-as-usual task. An incident response plan and a solid security policy are also essential tools to respond quickly and effectively to any potential threats while keeping your business PCI-DSS compliant.

Merchant Compliance Levels & Requirements

This chapter provided information on PCI-DSS compliance requirements for merchants and service providers. The levels of compliance are based on the number of card transactions processed annually, with four merchant levels and two service provider levels. Compliance can be determined through an external assessment by a Qualified Security Assessor (QSA) or Internal Security Assessor (ISA) for Level 1 organizations. At the same time, Levels 2-4 can conduct a self-assessment questionnaire (SAQ). It is vital to clearly understand the compliance level to determine the appropriate level of compliance and necessary audit or questionnaire approach.

Service Provider Compliance Levels

The Payment Card Industry Data Security Standard (PCI-DSS) categorizes service providers into two levels based on the number of transactions they process per year. Level one providers process more than 300k in annual transactions, while Level two providers process less than 300k annually. Service providers are businesses that handle cardholder data security and provide services like firewalls, hosting, and web gateway services. Level one service providers require a Report on Compliance (RoC), Attestation of Compliance (AOC), and ASV Scan, while level two only requires a Self-Assessment Questionnaire (SAQ) and ASV Scan.

Card Brand Service Provider Levels

I've discussed the importance of understanding the different service levels expected from service providers by card brands such as Mastercard, Visa, Discover, JCB, and AMEX. I suggest visiting the respective websites to provide you with a better understanding of their levels and requirements for PCI Compliance. I've provided the links to some of the card brand's websites for further information on their service provider levels.

Approved Scanning Vendor (ASV)

An Approved Scanning Vendor (ASV) is a company certified by the Payment Card Industry (PCI) Security Standards Council to offer vulnerability scanning services to identify and address security weaknesses in an organization's Cardholder Data Environment (CDE). ASVs have specific responsibilities and requirements, such as performing external vulnerability scans without interfering with the production environment, avoiding dangerous testing and providing a means for dispute resolution. The ASV must retain scan results for at least two years. To choose an ASV, look for companies on the PCI SSC's list of qualified vendors.

The Six Control Objectives

The PCI-DSS framework is vital for securing and protecting cardholder data. Implementing the proper security measures can reduce the risk of data breaches, but it is crucial to implement them correctly. The framework has six control objectives that organizations must adhere to ensure their payment cardholder data is secure and protected from malicious actors.

1: Build and Maintain Secure Networks and Systems | 2: Protect Account Data

3: Maintain a Vulnerability Management Program | 4: Implement Strong Access Control Measures

5: Test and Monitor All Network Systems | 6: Maintain a Security Policy

The 12 PCI-DSS Requirements

The content outlines essential measures to ensure network security and protect cardholder data. These measures include installing and maintaining security controls, applying secure configurations, using strong cryptography for data transmission, protecting against malicious software, developing secure systems and software, restricting access on a need-to-know basis, authenticating user access, restricting physical access to data, logging and monitoring all access, regularly testing security, and supporting information security with policies and programs.

1. Install and maintain network security controls

2. Apply secure configurations to All system components

3. Protect stored account data

4. Protect cardholder data with strong cryptography during transmission over open, public networks

5. Protect all systems and networks from malicious software

6. Develop and maintain secure systems and software

7. Restrict Access to system components and cardholder data on a 'Business Need To Know basis

8. Identify users and authenticate access to system components

9. Restrict physical access to cardholder data

10. Log and monitor All access to system components and cardholder data

11. Regularly test the security of systems and networks

12. Support information security with organizational policies and programs

Compensating Controls

To be clear, compensating controls can be used to reduce the risks associated with specific requirements, but only if they meet the same level of rigor and intent. Plus, they must provide a similar level of protection while offsetting risks the original requirement was designed to mitigate. Just keep in mind that for compensating controls to be valid, they must be reviewed by a PCI QSA. And don't think you can use them because you disagree with a PCI-DSS requirement. Compensating controls should only be used when a valid technical or business constraint prevents you from adhering to the original requirement.

The Appendix

The PCI-DSS has several appendices that provide additional requirements for multi-tenant service providers, entities using SSL/early TLS for card-present POS POI terminal connections, designated entities requiring supplemental validation, and organizations wanting to meet specific PCI DSS requirements in a customized way. The compensating controls worksheet includes areas such as constraints, definition of compensating controls, identified risks, and validation of compensating controls. Appendix F outlines how merchants and organizations can use custom software that follows the PCI SSC Secure Software Standard and Secure SLC Standard to meet secure systems and software requirements.

Self Assessment Questionnaires (SAQ's)

The PCI-DSS Self-Assessment Questionnaires (SAQs) are for merchants and service providers to guide them on their compliance journey. All of the SAQs are designed for different types of merchants and service providers and their cardholder data environments. These questionnaires require responses to various questions associated with specific requirements to ensure cardholder data security. The SAQs help you to state to your acquirer how you are complying with the PCI DSS. SAQ D is the only option if none of the other SAQs meet an organization's criteria.

AoC & RoC Compliance

The Payment Card Industry Data Security Standard (PCI-DSS) requires organizations to demonstrate compliance with its security requirements through an Attestation of Compliance (AoC) or a Report on Compliance (RoC). An AoC certifies a company's compliance with PCI-DSS and is completed by a Qualified Security Assessor (QSA). An RoC outlines an organization's security posture, environment, systems, and cardholder data protection. RoCs are required for all Level 1 merchants who process more than 6 million Visa or Mastercard transactions annually. After an audit, the QSA prepares an RoC, which must be presented to the merchant's acquirer and sent to the payment brand for verification.

Prioritized Approach Tool (PAT)

The Prioritized Approach Tool (PAT) helps organizations prioritize their compliance efforts by identifying quick wins and tracking progress against PCI-DSS controls. It aims to protect cardholder data and sensitive authentication data through security milestones. The tool helps identify gaps in compliance programs and areas that require focus. The PAT is ideal for PCIPs to prioritize activities and meet deadlines. Six areas are prioritized, including limiting data retention, protecting systems in case of a breach, securely accepting payment cards, monitoring system access, protecting cardholder data, and completing the remaining compliance efforts.

User Authentication and Password Security

To ensure the highest level of protection for your cardholder data, you must implement stringent security policies. Your password should be complex and changed at least once every 90 days. After ten failed attempts, lock out the user ID for at least 30 minutes or until an administrator enables it. Re-authenticate after an idle session of more than 15 minutes. Do not use commonly known passwords such as LetMeIn123 or Password1234. All non-console accesses to the CDE should be protected by multi-factor authentication, ensuring everyone with administrative access is held to the highest security standards.

The Exciting Journey of PCI DSS Changes: A Lifecycle Overview

The PCI-DSS has a 36-month lifecycle with eight stages, starting in October after the Council's annual Community Meetings. Organizations should transition to new standards quickly, especially for critical control requirements. Stakeholders can provide feedback during Stage 4 from November to March of Year 2. Stage 5 marks the official retirement of outdated PCI DSS standards on the last day of December in Year 2. Stage 6 happens from April through August of Year 2, and the final stage involves the review and adjustment of drafts by the Council and Board of Advisors from May through July of Year 3.

Additional Technology Information

This chapter discusses the importance of integrating PCI-DSS into business-as-usual processes and provides best practices for doing so. It emphasizes that PCI-DSS is more than just a yearly monitoring and testing process. It also highlights the importance of encrypting data in transit and mentions the potential risks associated with mobile payment acceptance. Topics included: Business As Usual (BAU), Network Segmentation, Tokenization, Virtualization, Point-to-Point-Encryption (P2PE), Mobile Devices, Wifi, Bluetooth (BT), Near Field Communication (NFC) and Biometric Authentication.

THE 10 BEST TIPS TO STUDY FOR THE PCIP EXAM

Studying can be a daunting task, but with the right approach, it can be an enjoyable and rewarding experience.

Here are 10 tips to help you study effectively:

1. **Set a goal:** Before you start studying, set a clear and achievable goal. This will help you stay focused and motivated throughout your study session.

2. **Create a schedule:** Plan your study sessions in advance and create a schedule that works for you. Make sure to include breaks and time for relaxation.

3. **Find a quiet place:** Choose a quiet and comfortable place to study where you won't be distracted by noise or other people.

4. **Eliminate distractions:** Turn off your phone, close unnecessary tabs on your computer, and avoid social media while studying.

5. **Take notes:** Taking notes is an effective way to retain information and helps you remember important points.

6. **Use visual aids:** Visual aids such as diagrams, charts, and graphs can help you understand complex concepts more easily.

7. **Practice active learning:** Engage in active learning by asking questions, summarizing what you've learned, and testing yourself.

8. **Take breaks:** Taking regular breaks can help prevent burnout and improve your overall productivity.

9. **Stay hydrated:** Drinking water can help improve brain function and keep you alert during long study sessions.

10. **Reward yourself:** After completing a study session or achieving a goal, reward yourself with something you enjoy, like watching your favorite show or treating yourself to a snack, or maybe going for a walk or run.

Remember, everyone has their unique way of studying that works best for them, so don't be afraid to try out different techniques until you find the one that clicks with you!

Disclaimer: It is vital that you read the PCI-DSS version 4.0 documents and supplemental documentation on the PCI SSC website to enable you to truly understand and pass the examination.

Top Tips for Your PCIP Test Day

Congratulations on taking the first step towards becoming a Payment Card Industry Professional (PCIP) v4.0! As you gear up for your exam day, let's review some helpful tips to make the process a breeze.

First and foremost, make sure you've completed all the necessary last-minute preparations. This includes checking that your computer and internet connection meet the pre-exam system requirements, clearing your workspace of any prohibited items, and having your ID ready to present. Reviewing the Pearson VUE Exam rules and testing advice for any specific guidelines is also a great idea.

On the day of your exam, be sure to start the check-in process up to 30 minutes before your appointment time. This will give you plenty of time to complete any necessary steps before beginning your exam.

Once you start your exam, staying focused on the questions and avoiding getting sidetracked is essential. Remember to follow all environmental and behavioral rules, such as staying at your desk and refraining from talking during the exam. If you need assistance during your exam, don't hesitate to use the chat icon to request help from a live proctor.

Tip: Within the test environment, you have access to a Whiteboard. Here you can make quick notes to help jog your memory. You will have memorized the Merchant Levels, Control Objectives

**and the 12 Requirements but jotting them down on the White-
board will help here.**

By following these helpful tips, you can ensure a smooth and successful experience while taking your PCIP exam from the comfort of your home or office. Best of luck!

PCI Resources

Welcome to the exciting world of PCI-DSS! Whether you're a seasoned expert or a fresh-faced PCIP student, the PCI Council website is an absolute goldmine of information waiting to be unearthed. Imagine stumbling upon a diamond in the rough, with resources that glitter and reveal the mysteries of PCI-DSS.

Make sure to check out the Document Library - it's a must-visit for anyone looking to gain knowledge and pass the PCIP exam. But don't think it's just for certification seekers! If your organization needs to comply with PCI-DSS, this library is an invaluable resource that you simply can't afford to miss.

The Document Library is jam-packed with an extensive collection of documentation, covering everything from specifications and tools to support resources. All of these resources are neatly organized for easy access, so you can quickly find what you need.

So what are you waiting for? Dive in today and discover all that this incredible resource has to offer - especially if you're eager to become a PCIP!

*Tip: When on the document resource page, select PCI-DSS version
4.0 from the dropdowns*

PCI Security Standards Council

https://www.pcisecuritystandards.org/

PCI SSC Blog

https://blog.pcisecuritystandards.org/

Training & Qualification Details

https://www.pcisecuritystandards.org/program_training_and_qualification/pci_profes
sional_qualification/

YouTube: You'll be thrilled to know that YouTube is a treasure trove of video resources dedicated to this topic. However, it's essential to ensure you're watching videos relevant to the PCI-DSS v4.0. Don't worry, with a little research, you'll be able to find the right videos in no time! So buckle up and get ready to dive into the exciting world of PCI-DSS!

Search for:

- Ingram Micro Cyber Security: PCI DSS Fundamentals.

- IT Governance have several videos about PCI DSS.

LinkedIn: Are you seeking high-quality video resources to enhance your understanding of PCI-DSS? Look no further than LinkedIn! This platform offers a plethora of informative and captivating content that can help you elevate your knowledge in no time. Although some of these resources necessitate a subscription to access, the investment is worthwhile for anyone committed to staying ahead of the game in this dynamic field. Don't hesitate any longer; register now and begin exploring all the valuable resources LinkedIn offers!

Check out the PCI-DSS v4.0 courses offered by Laura Louthan on LinkedIn Learning.

GLOSSARY

The PCIP certification is like a key to unlocking the world of information security in the context of a cardholder data environment. With this certification, you will be able to navigate the depths of the industry with confidence and ease.

The abbreviations below are like a map, guiding you through the winding roads and unfamiliar terrain. They will help you make sense of the jargon and technical language that can be so daunting to those who are new to the field. With a basic understanding of these abbreviations, you will be able to converse confidently with industry experts and stay ahead of the curve.

Below is a handy selection of acronyms along with their descriptions that you will come across while studying for the PCIP certification.

AIM = Access and Identity Management: Managing digital identities and access rights within an organization's network. This helps ensure secure user authentication, authorization, and audibility to reduce security risks.

AoC = Attestation on Compliance: A document that confirms an organization's adherence to the Payment Card Industry Data Security Standard (PCI DSS).

ASV = Application Scanning Vendor: A company certified by the PCI Security Standards Council to perform external vulnerability scans of a merchant's cardholder data environment.

CAV = Cardholder Authentication Verification: Verification process for cardholders' identity.

CDE = Cardholder Data Environment: The environment where cardholder data is stored, processed, or transmitted.

CHD = Cardholder Data: Sensitive information related to payment cards, such as account numbers and expiration dates.

CIA = Confidentiality, Integrity & Availability: The three pillars of information security - Confidentiality, Integrity & Availability.

CID = Card Identification Value: A unique value assigned to each payment card for identification purposes.

CPR = Code of Professional Responsibility: A set of ethical guidelines for professionals in the payment card industry.

CVC = Card Verification Code: Three-digit codes on payment cards used for verification purposes during transactions.

CVV = Card Verification Value: Three-digit codes on payment cards used for verification purposes during transactions.

DMZ = Demilitarised Zone: A Demilitarized Zone is a network security area that separates an internal network from an external one. It acts as a buffer zone to prevent unauthorized access to the internal network.

DNS = Domain Name System: A network segment that separates an organization's internal network from the internet.

DSS = Data Security Standard: A set of security standards established by the Payment Card Industry Security Standards Council (PCI SSC).

EMV = Europay, Mastercard and Visa: A global standard for credit and debit payment cards based on chip technology.

FTP = File Transfer Protocol: Protocols used for transferring files over the internet securely.

FW = Firewall: A network security system that monitors and controls incoming and outgoing traffic based on predetermined security rules.

HSM = Hardware Security Module: A physical device used to manage digital keys and perform cryptographic operations securely.

IDS = Intrusion Detection System: Systems that detect unauthorized access or attacks on computer networks.

IPS = Intrusion Prevention System: Systems that detect and prevent unauthorized access or attacks on computer networks.

ISA = Internal Security Assessor: Professionals certified by the PCI SSC to assess an organization's compliance with PCI DSS requirements.

JIT = Just In Time Access: JIT means Just In Time Access. It's a security method that allows users to access resources only when necessary, reducing the risk of unauthorized access and security breaches.

NTP = Network Time Protocol: A protocol used to synchronize computer clocks over a network.

P2PE = Point-to-Point Encryption: An encryption method used to protect payment card data during transmission from point-of-sale devices to processing systems.

SSF = Software Security Framework: The PCI Software Security Framework (SSF) is a set of rules and tools that help ensure payment software is designed and developed safely and securely.

PAN = Primary Account Number: The primary account number on a payment card.

PAT = Prioritised Approach Tool: A tool used to prioritize PCI DSS requirements based on an organization's risk level.

PCIP = Payment Card Industry Professional: Professionals certified by the PCI SSC with expertise in payment card security.

PIN = Personal Identification Number: A personal identification number used for authentication purposes during transactions.

PTS = Pin Transaction Standard: Standards established by the PCI SSC for secure PIN entry devices.

QSA = Qualified Security Assessor: Professionals certified by the PCI SSC to assess an organization's compliance with PCI DSS requirements.

RoC = Report on Compliance: A report that documents an organization's compliance with PCI DSS requirements.

SAD = Sensitive Authentication Data: Sensitive authentication data, such as full magnetic stripe data or PINs.

SAQ = Self Assessment Questionnaire: Self-assessment questionnaires used by merchants to assess their compliance with the PCI DSS.

SDLC = System Development Life Cycle or Software Development Life Cycle: The SDLC is a process developers use to create and maintain software & systems. It involves planning, analysis, design, implementation, testing, and maintenance stages. The SDLC aims to develop software & systems efficiently, effectively, and in accordance with end-users requirements.

SFTP = Secure File Transfer Protocol: Protocols used for securely transferring files over the internet.

SHA-1/SHA-2 = Secure Hash Algorithm: Secure Hash Algorithm is a cryptographic hash function used for data encryption and authentication. SHA-2 is an updated version of SHA-1, which provides stronger security.

SSC = Security Standards Council: Security Standards Council is an organization that develops and maintains standards for secure payment card transactions, known as the Payment Card Industry Data Security Standard (PCI DSS).

SSH = Secure Shell: Secure Shell is a protocol used for secure remote access to a computer or server. It encrypts data transmitted over the network to prevent unauthorized access.

SSL/TLS = Secure Socket Layer and Transport Layer Security: Secure Socket Layer and Transport Layer Security are protocols used for secure communication over the internet. They provide encryption and authentication of data transmitted between servers and clients.

TSP = Token Service Provider: Token Service Provider is a service that provides tokens for secure authentication and authorization of users in a system.

VLAN = Virtual Local Area Network: Virtual Local Area Network is a logical grouping of devices on a network, regardless of their physical location. It allows for better network management and security.

VPN = Virtual Private Network: Virtual Private Network is a secure connection between two networks over the internet. It provides privacy and security by encrypting data transmitted between them.

WAF = Web Application Firewall: A web Application Firewall is a security solution that protects web applications from attacks such as SQL injection, cross-site scripting, and other vulnerabilities.

WAN = Wide Area Network: Wide Area Network is a network that spans large geographical areas, connecting multiple local networks.

WEP/WPA/WPA2 = Wired Equivalent Privacy/WiFi Protected Access/WiFi Protected Access 2: Wired Equivalent Privacy/WiFi Protected Access/WiFi Protected Access 2 are wireless security protocols used to protect WiFi networks from unauthorized access. WPA2 is the most secure protocol among them.

ZT = Zero Trust: Zero Trust (ZT) is a security model that assumes no user or device can be trusted by default. It requires continuous identity verification and authorization before granting access to resources, minimizing the risk of data breaches and cyber attacks.

Tip: For a complete and extensive list, go to (https://pcisecuritys tandards.org) to view the Glossary of Terms, Abbreviations, and Acronyms.

AFTERWORD

'TRUST, BUT VERIFY'

Ronald Reagan's famous quote, "Trust, but verify," is a wise reminder that we should not blindly rely on someone's word alone. This principle is especially important in the context of PCI-DSS and credit cards.

In this context, "Trust, but verify" means that while we may trust that a company is compliant with PCI-DSS, we must also verify it through regular audits and assessments. This helps ensure that the company maintains the necessary security measures to protect sensitive credit card information.

For example, let's say you are a small business owner who accepts credit card payments. You have implemented all the necessary security measures to comply with PCI-DSS standards, and you believe your system is secure. However, you cannot simply assume that everything is working as it should be. You must regularly verify your compliance through assessments and audits conducted by qualified third-party assessors.

In conclusion, "Trust, but verify" is an essential principle in the world of PCI-DSS v4.0 and credit cards. It reminds us that we cannot take anything for granted when protecting sensitive information. By regularly verifying compliance with PCI-DSS standards, we can help ensure that our customers' credit card data remains safe and secure.

Tip: PCI-DSS (Payment Card Industry Data Security Standard) is a set of security standards designed to ensure that all companies that accept, process, store or transmit credit card information maintain a secure environment. Compliance with these standards is mandatory for any organization that handles credit card data.

Author Bio

John Meah

John is a freelance writer, a PCIP, CISSP & CCSK Certified Cybersecurity Consultant, and a Full Member of the Chartered Institute of Information Security (CIIS). He works for an international offshore bank and previously spent many years working in Automotive Security, with the last twenty years in IT & Information Security within the Banking, Financial, and Logistics service sectors.

He successfully implemented PCI-DSS and a Secure-SDLC, and manages security for all projects, including governance, compliance, system design choices, implementations, vendor relationships, and so much more.

Before having a cybersecurity career, John spent many years attending crime scenes, specifically automotive crime, picking up the pieces with Law Enforcement and other emergency services. Initially, working as a security product specialist and incident responder, then as an incident manager across central London.

'At a deep level, security has always been top of mind for me; it's in my nature to ask questions, be curious, and be vigilant. This 'Security Mindset' translates into Zero tolerance for any crime, especially cybercrime, and a Zero Trust by design viewpoint.'

Today, John writes content for Techopedia and multiple technology companies in the U.S. and Canada. He's been featured in the InfoSec Magazine and Writers & Artists.co.uk.

John's writing journey enables him to present the PCIP 4.0 Ultimate Study Guide from a practical, pragmatic, and resourceful viewpoint.

With a passion for creative writing, and a fascination for anything cyber-related, backed by his security background, his future projects include a cyber-thriller.